RISE AND FALL OF
PASTORS
IN THE 21ST CENTURY

Dr. Sharon D. Jones

Rise and Fall of Pastors in the 21st Century

Copyright © 2020 by Dr. Sharon D. Jones

Printed in the
United States of America

Published by Kingdom Publishing, LLC
Odenton, Maryland

All rights reserved. No part of this book may be reproduced or transmitted in any form of by any means, electronic or mechanical, including photocopying, recording or by any information storage and retrieval system without written permission from the author, excerpt for the inclusion of brief quotations in a review.

Scripture quotations are from the King James Version of the Bible (Thomas Nelson Publishers, Nashville: Thomas Nelson, Inc. 1972), Public Domain and New International Version of the Bible (Zondervan Publishing House, Michigan: The Zondervan Corporation, 1985), Public Domain. All rights reserved.

Editor: Dr. Diane Nixon
Copy Editor: Antonio Palmer
Cover Design: Kingdom Publishing
Cover Photo: Property of Dr. Sharon Jones
ISBN Paperback: 978-1-947741-57-7
ISBN Ebook - 978-1-947741-58-4
Library of Congress Control Number: 2020915021

ACKNOWLEDGEMENTS

First, all thanks and honor belong to my Heavenly Father. In 2016, You spoke in my heart to surrender control of my plans and to pursue a doctorate degree. Within three-and-a-half years, You helped me to successfully complete Logos University and publish this book. I am forever grateful for Your prompting!

Secondly, I thank my mother, Fannie Russell. You have always encouraged and supported me throughout life and ministry. You were the first person who challenged me to excel in life.

Thirdly, I thank all pastors, ministers, and lay members who contributed to my studies. Many of you responded in a moment's notice with candid and transparent answers.

May the Lord continue to abundantly bless you, your families, and your ministries.

DEDICATION

I dedicate this book to my pastor and husband,
Bishop Aaron R. Jones, DMin.

You truly have a shepherd's heart for God's sheep. Daily, you exemplify Matthew 18:12b: "...*doth he not leave the ninety and nine, and goeth into the mountains, and seeketh that which is gone astray?*"

PREFACE

For nearly twenty years, each day, one would hear or see in the news that a senior pastor has committed suicide, unexpectedly resigned, or was investigated for mismanagement of funds. Each time, I became heartbroken. I would grievously ask the Lord, "Why?" As ministers of the gospel, we are expected to provide hope in a hopeless society. We are expected to express joy in times of sorrow. We are expected to be physically and emotionally stable, even in our hardships. So, what has gone wrong? What is happening to the shepherds of God's sheep?

This book takes the journey from God's intent for pastors to individuals responding to the call to ministry; from ministerial training to ministry expectations; from the pastor's family to ministry highs and lows; and lastly, to the warning signs and the need for pastoral soul care. My prayer is that the pastor, who is reading this book, will see the threats, recognize warning signs, and seek soul care. Lastly, my prayer is that parishioners will proactively and earnestly pray for their pastors. The Apostle Paul encouraged the church in 1 Timothy 2:1-2, *"I exhort therefore, that, first of all, supplications, prayers, intercession, and giving thanks, be made for all men; for kings, and for all that are in authority; that we may lead a quiet and peaceable life in all godliness and honesty."*

TABLE OF CONTENTS

ACKNOWLEDGEMENTS iii

DEDICATION iv

PREFACE v

CHAPTER 1 - God's Intent for Pastors 1

CHAPTER 2 - Responding to the Pastoral Call 13

CHAPTER 3 - Ministerial Education, Training
              and Mentorship 27

CHAPTER 4 - The Expectations 47

CHAPTER 5 - The Pastor's Family 65

CHAPTER 6 - Pastoral Ministry Highs 81

CHAPTER 7 - Pastoral Ministry Lows 93

CHAPTER 8 - The Warning Signs 105

CHAPTER 9 - Pastoral Soul Care 121

CHAPTER 10 - Conclusion 137

BIBLIOGRAPHY 143

ABOUT THE AUTHOR 151

Chapter 1
GOD'S INTENT FOR PASTORS

Media reports of the immoral conduct of a prominent pastor, the suicide of a mega-church pastor, or a pastor's lavish living at the expense of the church heightened awareness of pastoral successes, failures, or demises. Such attention is causing a division in the body of Christ and a negative response from society. Hence, there is a need to examine, more fully understand, and recalibrate to God's original plan for shepherds.

Addressed in this book is the question of the rise and fall of pastors in the 21st century and the threats that cause a decline in leadership. Presented are biblical, theological, and practical principles to equip pastors with an awareness of the threats that cause a decline in leadership. Included is an assessment of society's misunderstanding, misconception, and misinterpretation of the role of the pastor, as these concepts pertain to a pastor's rise and fall.

Primary data stemmed from interviews and questionnaires to survey pastors and their family members, administrators, church members, and professional counselors who informed this research. Findings, derived from peer-reviewed literature, published articles, and statistics from 2000 to present, illustrate pastoral successes and failures. The results of this book equip pastors to embrace their shepherd's call, to be aware of leadership threats, and to encourage pastoral soul care.

An exploration of God's intent for pastors begins this book's journey. There are various descriptions of a pastor, but God is the original human resource Person who designed the position. The heartbeat of God is the souls He created. He characterizes these souls as His sheep. Throughout Scripture, one would see God reference His people as sheep. The psalmist states, *"Know ye that the Lord He is God: it is He that hath made us, and not we ourselves; we are His people, and the sheep of His pasture"* (Psalm 100:3). One can observe and assess that God is deliberate in the care of His sheep and that pastors are His shepherds. Additional pastoral assignments performed are added benefits to building God's kingdom. For centuries, people viewed the role of the pastor as a servant caregiver. As the years and ministries progressed, the pastor's role transformed and advanced from servant-leader to chief executive officer (CEO). In this chapter, there is an exploration of God's intent for pastors, based on these various ideologies, leading to a discussion of the perspectives derived from the interviews of five senior pastors who are currently active in leading their ministries.

Pastors as Shepherds

God has created many animals and species. Why would He liken us to sheep? Sheep have many characteristics that are similar to mankind. Just to name a few, they display an arguable lack of intelligence. They are directionless, restless, needy, and sensitive.

Lack of Intelligence

Sheep are not known to be smart or cunning animals when it comes to safety. Rather, they are susceptible, and they tend to wander away from the protection of the shepherd. People are not inherently unintelligent, but they do tend to wander away from God, and from everything that is right and holy.[1]

Directionless

Sheep get lost easily, and so it is with those outside of the Lord. There is simply no sense of spiritual direction in their lives. They cannot find their way to the Lord by themselves.[2]

Restless

Sheep become restless because of hunger. They become restless when food is scarce. An individual who hasn't eaten after a period of time becomes anxious and oftentimes disgruntled; it is difficult and cumbersome to communicate with people who are unsettled because of hunger. Individuals become spiritually hungry when the word of God is lacking.[3]

Needy

Sheep need someone to protect them. They must stay close to the shepherd. People are spiritually weak, and they need THE Shepherd to care for them.[4]

Sensitive

Sheep respond to and follow the shepherd's voice. The voice of the shepherd brings comfort and security to the sheep. Individuals may never have a complete understanding of their circumstances, but they will understand the love of God and the importance of following him.[5]

Collective Traits

One can identify with each of these traits. Some may think that children are the only ones who are needy, but the state of necessity is no respecter of person. Whether one is a Christian or not, people have the tendency to lack the understanding required to adapt to their environments or circumstances, and are generally in need of someone to instruct or give guidance in life. Everyone needs to be protected from outside dangers, as well as inside dangers (i.e. oneself). Although some individuals may believe that they function well alone, mostly everyone appreciates the love and care shown towards them. Lastly, people are familiar with the voices of loved ones and friends. They will immediately react and respond to that which is familiar, and ignore a stranger who is vying for their attention.

Shepherding the Sheep

God has always protected and provided for His sheep. According to these human and spiritual attributes, His intent for pastors is to serve as shepherds and to tend to His sheep. However, there are 28 Bible verses about inadequate shepherding.[6] Dr. Bruce Rosdahl noted from Psalm 23 and John 10 that God's resolve for each inadequate shepherding was that He would rescue His people.[7] He would search for them and bring them home. He would care and restore them. He would lead them to green pastures and give them rest. *Holman Bible Dictionary* defined a pastor as a shepherd or one who keeps animals, used figuratively for those called by God to feed, care for, and lead His people, who are His flock.[8]

Feed

God's intent for shepherds was to feed the sheep or provide the sheep with knowledge and understanding of Him. *"And I will give you pastors according to mine heart, which shall feed you with knowledge and understanding"* (Jeremiah 3:15). Additional Scriptures provide numerous examples of God's intention for pastors to feed His sheep. *"And I will set up shepherds over them which shall feed them: and they shall fear no more, nor be dismayed, neither shall they be lacking, saith the Lord"* (Jeremiah 23:4).

During this time period, the priests, rulers, and prophets had been negligent in their relationship with God. The rulers were referred to as shepherds.[9] In their negligence, the sheep were feasting from the heathen nations and adapting to their culture of idol worship. Such conduct was an abomination to God. Therefore, God had to remind and redirect the leaders concerning their shepherding obligations—to feed the sheep. If a parishioner (a sheep) is lacking in the truths of God's word, it is the pastor's responsibility to teach (feed) it. According to Jesus, a pastor displays His love for Him by teaching (feeding) His sheep.

Care

One can observe and assess that God is deliberate in the care of His sheep. God's intent for pastors is to care for His sheep with willing hearts and not for selfish gain. He never presented the shepherd's role as a job with material benefits. God declared the role of caretaker as a representation of Him and His unfailing love. Scriptures provide numerous examples of God's intention for pastors to care for His sheep:

> *"But he that is a hireling, and not the shepherd, whose own the sheep are not, seeth the wolf coming, and leaveth the sheep, and fleeth: and the wolf catcheth them, and scattereth the sheep. The hireling fleeth, because he is an hireling, and careth not for the sheep. I am the good shepherd, and know my sheep, and am known of mine"* (John 10:12-14).

A hireling is someone with a mercenary interest in the job for which he has been hired.[10]

Jesus emphasized caring for the sheep wasn't a job, but a desire. His care for God's people was likened to a shepherd watching after His sheep. Jesus explained, when a shepherd sees trouble headed toward the sheep, he protects them, unlike a hireling, who would run and protect himself first. Jesus made known that a good shepherd would not allow harm, because it isn't a job, but a love for the sheep.

The Apostle Peter charged the elders to feed the flock of God which is among you, taking the oversight thereof, not by constraint, but willingly; not for filthy lucre, but of a ready mind (1 Peter 5:2). Dr. Rosdahl stated, "When our leadership does not exemplify Christ, we give people a distorted view of God. When the church has been a place of hurt, people leave to look elsewhere for hope."[11] The unfortunate outcome is sheep, in search of care, are turning to hirelings and away from the Good Shepherd, Jesus Christ.

Lead

God's intent for pastors as shepherds is to lead His sheep in the path of safety, provision, and wholeness. Sheep follow the guidance of their shepherd. *"To him the porter openeth; and the sheep hear his voice: and he calleth his own sheep by name, and leadeth them out. And when he putteth forth his own sheep, he goeth before them, and the sheep follow"* (John 10:3-4). Additional scriptures provide numerous examples of God's intention for pastors to care for and lead His sheep:

> *"As a shepherd seeketh out his flock in the day that he is among his sheep that are scattered; so will I seek out my sheep, and will deliver them out of all places where they have been scattered in the cloudy and dark day. And I will bring them out from the people, and gather them from the countries, and will bring them to their own land, and feed them upon the mountains of Israel by the rivers, and in all the inhabited places of the country"* (Ezekiel 34:12-13).

The role of the pastor is to keep the sheep from scattering into destructive areas, such as those areas that will spiritually deplete instead of spiritually add to their Christian lives. God's intent for pastors is to lead by example. If the pastor has an intimate relationship with Christ, the sheep will learn to develop an intimate relationship with Him. Sheep are always totally dependent on their shepherd. The sheep hear, respond, and follow the shepherd's voice. If the pastor is scattered, the sheep will scatter as well.

Servant Caregiver

There are various descriptions of a pastor, but God is the original human resource Person who designed the position. Any additional pastoral assignments performed are added benefits to building God's kingdom. Joseph Kidder stated that throughout the centuries, people viewed the role of pastor as servant caregivers who engage in:

- Teaching/preaching of traditional doctrine;
- Caregiving (such as visitation, counseling, and taking care of people's needs);
- Performing rites of passages (such as baptisms, wedding, and funerals);
- Administrating (such as meetings, bulletins, programs);
- Serving as ambassador of the church to the community.[12]

In the Old Testament, due to the lack of faithful shepherds and spiritual leaders, God warned that He will set up one who will be committed to the care of His sheep. The one is Jesus, the Son of God:

"And I will set up shepherds over them which shall feed them: and they shall fear no more, nor be dismayed, neither shall they be lacking, saith the Lord. Behold, the days come, saith the Lord, that I will raise unto David a righteous Branch, and a King shall reign and prosper, and shall execute judgment and justice in the earth. In his days Judah shall be saved, and Israel shall dwell safely: and this is His name whereby He shall

be called, The Lord Our Righteousness" (Jeremiah 23:4-6).

Jesus is the true example of a shepherd. He had a servant's heart. As the Son of God, He did not become human to be served, but to serve. He told the disciples that the greatest among them shall be a servant (Matthew 23:11). God's intent for pastors is servant leadership. In *Leading Like Jesus,* Ken Blanchard and Phil Hodge stated, "For followers of Jesus, servant leadership isn't an option; it's a mandate."[13] The role of the pastor was never intended to be a glorified, self-seeking responsibility. God's intention was self-sacrificing servants, who had tender hearts for His sheep.

When interviewing four lay members and two church leaders about their pastoral expectations, I asked them to describe their pastor's leadership styles as servant, leader, or servant-leader. All six stated that their pastors were servant-leaders. They emphasized that the people always see their pastor doing team ministry. A male lay member stated, "My pastor is a servant doing whatever jobs or assignment needed to be completed (especially if there's no one else to do it). He maintains an air of humility and friendliness that crosses various barriers." A male church leader likened his pastor's servant leadership to Mark 10:45, *"For even the Son of Man did not come to be served, but to serve, and to give his life a ransom for many."*

Servant pastors are more people-driven versus program-driven. Servant pastors are compassionate versus competitive. Servant pastors teach biblical principles versus charismatic topics. Servant pastors remain faithful to God's original plan for shepherds. Their desire and attraction to do more must have a proper balance, to remain Christ-seeking instead of self-seeking.

Changing Views of Pastors

As years and ministries progressed, the pastor's role transformed and advanced from a servant-leader to functioning as the CEO. Today, some pastors have little to no pastoral care involvement with their parishioners. Visitations and counseling are now conducted by additional staff ministers and lay-persons. It is stated that those who hold the view of pastors as CEO claim that the "pastor as shepherd" view threatens to stunt growth of a church and is impractical for the challenges of our day.[14] This perspective is paradoxical to God's original intention for pastors and can have consequences detrimental to the well-being of pastors themselves.

The Fuller Institute of Church Growth surveyed some Protestant pastors from a variety of denominations in America in 1991 and 2005. Their research reported that 75% of pastors are extremely stressed or highly stressed.[15] It is understood that caring for people may take a toll on one's heart. Understanding this fact requires self-introspection, seminary training, accountability partners, and more. The list can be exhaustive. The same research revealed that 70% of pastors say they have a lower self-esteem now than when they entered ministry.[16] These are alarming statistics that require more research and current assessment, which also prompt the following types of questions: What is the cause of this extreme stress and lower self-esteem? How does God's intended plan for pastors cause such emotional stress on individuals?

In a search for answers, I questioned five senior pastors (four men and one woman) about their definition and views of pastors and God's intention. Three are Protestant pastors and two are Christian network pastors (non-denomination). Their years of serving as senior pastor ranged from two years to twenty-three years at the time of the interviews. Four of the five pastors shepherded more than one church, located in the Washington, D.C. metropolitan communities, with a demographic audience of urban, suburban, and rural congregants. They ministered to diverse cultures and generational cohorts.

I was interested in knowing if their definition and view of pastoring changed after serving for numerous years. Before serving as a pastor, definitions encompassed the view of a pastor as one tasked to watch over the sheep and to feed them the word of God. After serving as pastors, definitions changed. All agreed that watching over the sheep and delivering the word of God is only a portion of the required task of the Senior Pastor. There was a consensus that the role of the pastor expanded to additional areas, such as executive leadership, human resource management, life coaches, and advisers.

Four of the five pastors interviewed believed there are many pastors who are fulfilling the call as God intended. They had a resounding voice that unfortunately there are some who have placed a faulty witness of pastoring in the Christian faith. One pastor believed many are not fulfilling the role because of faulty models and systems. He stated, "The systems tends to be geared to a corporate model and is effective, but lacks spiritually and is ineffective or vice versa." It is a consistent understanding as ministers that God's original and primary intention for pastors is to shepherd His sheep. Any additional responsibilities as a pastor are benefits to building God's kingdom, but should not be a priority.

Dr. Ruben Exantus stated that the ministry of the pastor is to shepherd the flock of God. "A shepherd is a person who cares for a flock of sheep. He has the responsibility to feed and lead them safely."[17]   I concur with Dr. Exantus that the pastor is a direct link to God and God's wishes.[18] God's wish and intention is to feed, protect, and lead His sheep at all times. One of the Protestant pastors concluded that he is thankful that God looks at the heart of the pastor, because when he felt he had an unsuccessful day in ministry, God was still with him. This encouraged him to stay motivated to keep on ministering to and shepherding people (whether received or rejected). I conclude this chapter from Dr.

God's Intent for Pastors

Exantus' words to pastors in Central Florida and around the world:

> "The ability to lead the flock of God is the greatest privilege ever given to man. Pastoring is a gift and you happen to be a gift that God gives to a church. God had something in His mind when He gave you the gift of pastor. It was to equip, edify, and nurture His people, the flock until we all come to the unity of the faith and of the knowledge of the Son of God. Pastoring is truly the highest privilege. But sometimes pastors can be the most misunderstood people in the church. Just remember, pastoring is not a job. It is a gift. You can be fired from a job, but nobody can take away your gift. Your gift is eternal."[19]

Endnotes

1. "Why does God call us sheep?," For His Service, 16 Apr. 2011, 6 Aug. 2019 http://inhonotoftheking.blogspot.com/2011/04/why-does-god-call-us-sheep.html?m=1, 1.
2. Ibid, 2.
3. Ibid, 3.
4. Ibid, 2.
5. Ibid, 3.
6. Inadequate Shepherding," Knowing Jesus, 27 Jul. 2019 https://bible.knowing-Jesus.com/topics/inadequate-Shepherding
7. Bruce Rosdahl, Ph.D., "Abusive Shepherds: God's Anger Over His Battered Flock," SAGU, 15 Dec. 2015, 27 Jul. 2019 https://www.sagu.edu/thoughthub/abusive-shepherds, 2.
8. *Holman Illustrated Bible Dictionary* (Nashville: Holman Bible Publishers, 2003) 1250.
9. Paul Alexander, "Lessons in Shepherding 2: Jeremiah and Ezekiel," 9Marks, 26 Feb. 2010, 27 Jul. 2019 https://www.9marks.org/article/lessons-shepherding-2-Jeremiah-and-Ezekiel/, 1.
10. *The New Webster's Comprehensive Dictionary of the English Language, Deluxe Edition* (New York: American International Press, 1990) 459.
11. Rosdahl, 2.
12. S. Joseph Kidder, DMin, "The bible role of the pastor," 26 Oct. 2009 11 Aug. 2019 https://www.ministrymagazine.org/archive/009/04/the-biblical-role-of-the-pastor, 2.
13. Ken Blanchard and Phil Hodges, *Lead Like Jesus*, (Nashville: Thomas Nelson, 2005) 12.
14. "What's the Purpose of Pastors?" Challies, 6 Oct. 2017, 11 Aug. 2019 https://www.challies.com/articles/what's-the-purpose-of-pastors/, 1.
15. Bill Gaultiere, "Pastor Stress Statistics," 12 Aug. 2019 https://www.soulshepherding.org/pastors-under-stress/, 2.
16. Ibid., 3.
17. W. Ruben Exantus, Ph.D., *Pastoral Burnout and Leadership Styles*, (Bloomington: AuthorHouse, 2012) 28.
18. Ibid., 40.
19. Ibid., 106-109.

Chapter 2

RESPONDING TO THE PASTORAL CALL

The initial call to ministry can be frightening, yet exciting. It is frightening because one is thinking, "Why would God want me to speak and represent Him?" One may think about present inadequacies and past failures, feeling unworthy to be used by God. The call can be exciting, because one is thinking, "I am amazed that God wants me to speak and represent Him!" One's mind begins to race with anticipation of the many opportunities that may be afforded to share the gospel. The Apostle Paul says, *"I thank Christ Jesus our Lord, who hath enabled me, for that He counted me faithful, putting me into the ministry"* (1 Timothy 1:12). Accordingly, only those who believe to be chosen by God, to become enabled in faith and the ministry, proceed to undertake this sacred task.

Call to the Pastorate

The call to ministry is an honorable experience. The call to the pastorate is humbling. The role of the pastor is connected to shepherding. Shepherds are responsible for their sheep. All ministry assignments entail people, but the pastor is more intimate and involved with the people served. An evangelist is devoted to preaching the gospel.[1] The pastor is devoted to preaching the gospel, discipling the parishioners, administrating the church functions, visiting the sick, and administering sacraments, among other responsibilities. The evangelist's ministry assignment may end immediately after preaching. The pastor's ministry assignment continues after preaching. Often times, the pastor is called to serve a few more hours after arriving home.

Some look at the role of a pastor and assume it is a glorified position. They may base this on what is seen in media. As the saying goes, "Everything is not as it seems." There is a plethora of responsibilities a pastor faces prior to standing before the congregation, and a torrent of events that occurs after preaching. Thus, some admit they were never called, claiming they felt led to enter the ministry because it offered the best platform for instituting economic, racial, political and social programs.[2] Those who truly received the pastoral call understand that the pulpit is not for personal gain, but for God's glory.

As stated in Chapter 1, God's intent for pastors is to feed and lead His sheep. He or she is a representation of the unconditional and uncompromising love of God. This chivalrous assignment, if not called by God, can be paralyzing to an individual. Ben Patterson claimed, "A call is not a career. It has no maps, no itinerary to follow, and no destination to envision. Careers lend themselves to formulas and blueprints."[3] When God calls an individual to ministry, at times, it is unexpected. Sometimes, it is at an inopportune time. One may sense a feeling of discomfort and uncertainty, because God does not provide details all at once. In a career, individuals may have dreamt about it as a child. He or she attended schools to prepare for the career. Most people have a general idea of the details that entail the career. This doesn't hold true when you are called by God.

Bishop Will Willimon shared a conversation he had with a young man who was prayerfully considering becoming a Methodist pastor. A concern of the young man and his wife was the meager salary on which they would have to live. They viewed it as a challenge because they were used to an affluent lifestyle since childhood.[4] When God calls one to the pastorate, He never mentions money and material benefits. God instills the desire to impart His word and to nurture His sheep, but the conversation about finances is rarely discussed.

This sparse conversation about finances is not to say that pastors are to shepherd for free, but to provide a clear understanding of the weight of the call. In the biography of one of the Church of God's former general overseer, Bishop Raymond Crowley, the writer noted, "In 1934, his beginning weekly salary as a pastor ranged from $10 to $12. His membership's average attendance was in the twenties. The church began to grow through Raymond's evangelistic preaching and pastoral visits."[5] The Apostle Paul had addressed hard work and freedom from the love of money with the Ephesian elders: *"In everything I showed you that by working hard in this manner you must help the weak."* He also reminded them of the words of the Lord Jesus, who said Himself that *"It is more blessed to give than to receive"* (Acts 20:33-35).

The instruction Paul had was to discontinue the persecution of Christians and to become a spokesperson for Christ. He was to declare God's unfailing love and grace for the Gentiles. Paul was also informed that his assignment wasn't going to be easy, but costly. The Lord said about Paul, *"Go thy way… a chosen vessel unto me, to bear my name before the Gentiles, and kings, and the children of Israel. For I will shew him how great things he must suffer for my name's sake"* (Acts 9:15-16). One may ask: With such limited and painful information, why would anyone choose to respond to the call of God? Wouldn't you want to do something a little more enjoyable and less threatening? Dr. James Berkley claimed that responding to the call is a holy ambition. Holy ambition appears as a desire to do all for Christ, to elevate him, to deny self and enjoy the freedom and fulfillment of doing God's will.

Holy ambition even encompasses humbly accepting perceived failures, if it will further God's purposes.[6] The key point is "to further God's purposes." Ministry is serving God's people and fulfilling His plan on Earth. His ultimate plan is reconciling mankind back to Him (2 Corinthians 5:19). Due to the disobedience of Adam and Eve, mankind's intimate relationship with God had been severed (Genesis 2:16-17). God's solution to reuniting Himself with mankind was His son, Jesus Christ (John 3:16). Thus, God's plan of reconciliation needed to be made known; therefore, He established pastors—men and women who share His heart for the sheep. Chaplain Craig Kocher describes God's call as "the subtle movement of the Spirit."[7] The individual is called to a deep communion with God.

One's acceptance of the pastoral calling means a "yes" to God and fearlessly abandoning anything that does not work toward His ends.[8] The role of the pastor, in relations to the plan, is to teach and to nurture God's sheep. This leaves no room for selfish gains and motives. The pastor's daily drive is to seek ways to urge God's sheep to stay in relationship with Him. Accordingly, God gives the pastor a heart for the people. Most pastors are attentive and compassionate. God gives them the ability to listen and discern. Pastor John Piper shared his testimony as he celebrated thirty years of pastoral ministry. He stated, during his sabbatical from working as a seminary professor, he sensed an increased longing to address a flock week after week and tried to draw them in to an experience of God that gives them more joy in Him than they have in anything else and thus magnifies Christ.[9]

A Calling for God's Purpose

The call of the pastor is more than a weekly assignment. One would find oneself serving God's people on a daily basis. Some assume that the only role of the pastor is to preach a sermon on Sunday, and maybe teach a mid-week Bible lesson. Preaching and teaching is only 20% of the pastoral assignment. The other 80% consists of visitations, administration, counseling, evangelism, community involvement, and more. Harold Westing identifies these assignments as a pastor's priorities.[10] Although preaching and teaching are forefront ministry assignments, they require hours and days of preparation before presenting to the congregation. The sermons and lessons spoken are from the heart of God. It is God's love message to His sheep. Therefore, quality time and preparation are crucial to a pastor. Pastor Williams Banks encourages pastors to always begin your sermons, Bible study, lectures, and the like with prayer. Ask the Lord's blessing upon your efforts and for Holy Spirit guidance.[11]

Bearing this in mind, the pastor must always remember that the call is to further God's purposes, not one's own. When the pastorate revolves around self and not God, it becomes devastating to the body of Christ and hence, the cause of sheep going astray. Vasile Filat stated, "If the sermons are not well planned and prepared, the saints will suffer, and the work of the church will decrease."[12] The Scriptures are the products of the infinitely wise, omniscient movement of God; accordingly, there is much more depth of meaning than any human being will ever be able to understand, Therefore, planning and preparation requires time with God's Word, while consciously in the presence of Him, asking to see His Word purposefully and rightly, to impart proper applications to life.

Some 21st century pastors have been declaring the cliché statement, "Being Real!" This term means that today's audience are not interested in traditional Biblical teachings. They want real, down-to-earth, relative to today, preaching and teaching. It has been said, "Pastors often face identity crises as the church succumbs to cultural and secular pressures as well as religious unrest."[13] Therefore, these pastors preach from the hip, as if they are in a western gun-fight with no preparation for REAL spiritual warfare. They provide more of their personal testimonies with no Biblical substance. Jesus said, *"Heaven and earth will pass away, but my words will never pass away"* (Mark 13:31). Scriptures were written to be understood, lived out, and appreciated. *"His delight is in the law of the LORD, and in his law he meditates day and night"* (Psalm 1:2). There is a need for Scriptural understanding and meaning that requires every pastor to meditate day and night.

God's word transcends time. He is also a relational and generational God. *"Know therefore that the Lord your God is God; He is the faithful God, keeping His covenant of love to a thousand generations of those who love Him and keep His commands"* (Deuteronomy 7:9).

Throughout Scripture, one sees God's consistent involvement with all generations. *"I was young and now I am old, yet I have never seen the righteous forsaken or their children begging bread"* (Psalm 37:25). Jesus Christ is *"the same yesterday, and today, and forever"* (Hebrews 13:8). The entire Bible, rightly understood, is internally and timelessly consistent. It does not lack in intergenerational teachings.

Yet, in four large, nationally representative surveys of over 11 million people, American adolescents and emerging adults at the beginning of the 21st century (Millennials) were significantly less religious than the Baby Boomers and Generation X of the same ages in previous generations. Twice as many reported no religious affiliation as in previous generations. However, the majority of adolescents and emerging adults remain religiously involved, although a large portion never attended religious services, disapprove of religious organizations, and spend little time praying or meditating. Declines in religious orientation were consistent across religious groups and were largest among girls, non-minorities, lower-socioeconomic classes, and in the Northeastern United States. Conclusions drawn in this and similar studies was that relatively lower religious orientation of Millennials, in comparison to previous generations, is due to time period or generation, and not to age or Biblical substance.[14]

In contrast to such findings, the significant debate about trends in religious orientation among generations of Americans continues with other studies showing contradictory results. For example, while several studies indicated that the percentage of adults reporting "none" for religious affiliation increased, other studies showed that religious service attendance, belief in God, and prayer did not decrease significantly and actually increased over the periods of recent timeframes studies.[15] Thus, variation in generational trends are based on specific aspects of religiosity, demographics, and the timeframes examined.

Within the context of preparation in response to God's calling, I questioned a Generation Xer, a Millennial, and two Centennial Christians on their thoughts about and reactions to someone preaching to them who appears to be unprepared. The Generation Xer stated that universally, he doesn't want any instruction from anyone that is unorganized or unprepared on any topic. The Millennial said, "I would feel that the person did not seek the Holy Spirit before preaching to me. A preacher can preach from the human spirit, as well as the Holy Spirit, but the Holy Spirit should always trump the human." One Centennial said, "It would depend on how obvious it is, the person's heart, and how well she knows the individual." She stated if such delivery is continuous or a nonchalant attitude is being displayed, she would feel more conflicted about sympathizing with the preacher. The other Centennial who is fourteen-years-old said:

> I would wonder if the preacher authentically received his or her words from the Lord or if that word is from his or her heart. I would also feel the need to conduct research on the preacher's sources or Scripture verses to gain interpretation of the intended meaning. Lastly, I would wonder, did the

preacher really care about the audience and chose to preach an unorganized message? I know no one is perfect, but it's still God's people. This shouldn't be taken lightly. I would imagine that being unsaved and hearing an unorganized message would create even more dissatisfaction and resentment.

It is interesting to observe the differences in generational responses. A Generation Xer and a Centennial have little tolerance. They are unwilling to receive unprepared preaching. The Millennial has minimal tolerance, but is willing to receive it, whereas the other Centennial will tolerate and accept it, if there are acceptable variables contributing to the lack of preparation. Rev. Jason Allen noted, "Get the 'I' out of the sermon. You will likely overestimate how much the congregation want to hear about you. They want to hear from you, but not so much about you."[16] Again, God's intent for pastors is to feed His sheep and to lead them to Him.

Pastoral Priorities

Quite often, as a pastor, there are times when he or she is unable to spend several days and hours to prepare a sermon or lesson. This is due to the additional pastoral priorities that Westing mentioned. Sometimes, church administration can consume a large percentage of the pastor's week, especially without an administrative assistant or church clerk. All pastors do not have the benefit of having additional office help. Churches with small congregations may not have the funding to hire two paid staff, the pastor, and an assistant. At the same time, the church may not have interested volunteers offering their services. Therefore, the pastor functions as executive leadership and secretary.

Church administration is a spiritual service requiring the wise stewardship of God's resources; administration is not an end but a means to the effective service and use of resources to best glorify God and lead His sheep. Pastor Paul Chappell stated, "Administration is not one of the top skills most people think of when they think of the responsibilities of the pastorate…But administration is necessary to the work of the Lord."[17] There are some pastors who view administrative duties as menial and not spiritual. They are charismatic speakers with amiable personalities, but they are disorganized and lack follow-up. This can be frustrating for the pastor and membership, because pertinent ministry matters may fall by the wayside.

Then, there are others who are strong administrators and spend extreme hours on the planning and implementing of programs, as well as managing the church's finances. This descriptive is my senior pastor. Although we have two part-time administrative assistants, a Finance Pastor, three part-time finance clerks, and a Human Resource Pastor, he still involves himself in the daily administrative functions. The reason is not because he is needed. Administration is one of his strongest gifts. Daily, we as an administration team encourage him to focus on the feeding and the leading, and trust us with the remainder. Sometimes, he distances himself and other times, he is working with us. Lastly, there are some who lack administrative and organizational skills. Hence, the need for an individual's assistance. Some retired and available members seek opportunities to volunteer at the church. It requires the pastor to make known and announce the need for administrative support.

Another pastoral priority that consumes his or her time is counseling and personal-spiritual growth development sessions with members. Surprisingly, not all pastors have good people skills. They may be great orators, but flawed in one-on-one communication. Some may do well providing Biblical principles, but error in personal counseling. Dr. Exantus stated:

"Spiritually, pastors are not sufficient for the task given to them. They never have been. They never will be...The human problem is too big, human nature is too disabled, and human beings are perverse. So, pastors need to be ready for the requirements for pastoral ministry in the 21st century."[18]

There is a senior pastor who doesn't hesitate to say, "I love to preach and teach, but counseling is not one of my strong spiritual gifts." His ministry has several locations and over 5,000 members. His pastoral staff does the counseling. Some would form a judgment and frown upon this pastor, but in actuality, he would be a hindrance to the body of Christ. Quite often, people are operating outside of their gifts and become agitated, dysfunctional, and burn out. They are operating outside of their pastoral call and the church suffers.

In a search for validation of Westin's list of pastoral priorities, I had six senior pastors (four men and two women) assess the percentage of time used to fulfill each responsibility in any given month. They are all Protestant pastors, with durations serving as senior pastor ranging from one to twenty-one years. Five pastors shepherded one church and one shepherded two churches. Two are bi-vocational pastors. One oversees several churches. The findings were that leading worship and preaching comprised no more than 30% of the pastoral duties identified by respondents, with the average among the pastors representing an even lower percentage of time invested into pastoral duties. Equally time-consuming was administration and counseling, followed by teaching, visitations, and coordinating programs for personal and spiritual growth. Consuming relatively smaller amounts of the pastoral time were duties as community and denominational leaders, enabling church members, and evangelism outside of the church membership, although all pastors surveyed reported some time spent with these activities.

In summary, God's calling is to those with sincerity of heart, and holy reverence of Him (Colossians 3:22). The Apostle Paul advised: *"Whatever you do, work heartily, as to the Lord and not to men, knowing that from the Lord you will receive the reward of the inheritance; for you serve the Lord Christ"* (Colossians 3:23–24). Even in the midst of such an emotionally taxing position of Christian leadership, the eternal reward is humbly serving the Lord Jesus Christ. *"If anyone aspires to the office of overseer, he desires a noble task"* (1 Timothy 3:1). God calls people who will do the work of ministry, and who will respond to the calling out of obedience and not as a sense of duty. Christ wants those who aspire to shepherd (pastor) the flock *"not under compulsion, but willingly"* (1 Peter 5:2). Pastoring ideally emerges from a call to aspiration and desire, not an appeal to obligation and duty. Although desire may emerge at the start of a pastoral calling, it does not replace a realistic understanding of the hard work and the emotional, spiritual and physical investment that the calling requires.

God's call is not just bringing one's aspiration and desires to a hurting society or community; but it means reconciling mankind back to Him. Some pastors may delight in this hard labor of love, and others may grow and experience real accomplishments; but there are many who find pleasure in meeting the needs of others which affirms their pastoral gifts and efforts. I conclude with Rev. Banks' advice to new pastors:

> Those 'not sent but who just went' can never experience the joy of having had a supernatural call into a supernatural ministry, or the joy of answering that calling, no matter how successful they may be from man's point of view. The calling to the Christian ministry is one of grace.[19]

Endnotes

1. Josie Sison Livingstone, "The Duties of an Evangelist," Classroom 29 Sept. 2017, 24 Aug. 2019 https://classroom.synonym.com/the-duties-of-an-evangelist-12080929.html.
2. William L. Banks, *Pastor's Pal* (Fort Washington: CLC Publications, 2007) 5.
3. James D. Berkley, General Editor, *Leadership Handbook of Management and Administration* (Grand Rapids: Baker Books, 14) 1994.
4. Craig T. Kocher, Jason Byassee, and James C. Howell, Editors, *Mentoring For Ministry: The Grace of Growing Pastors* (Eugene: CASCADE Books, 2017) 51.
5. Philip and Mary Morris, *Uncharted Waters: The Life & Ministry of Raymond E. Crowley* (Cleveland: Pathway Press, 2014) 51.
6. Berkley, 23.
7. Kocher, 96.
8. Natasha Sistrunk Robinson, "Answering the Call of God," ChristianityToday.com Jan. 2013, 24 Aug. 2019 https://www.christianitytoday.com/women-leaders/2013/January/answering-call-of-god.html?paging+off
9. Justin Taylor, "30 Years Ago Today: How God Called John Piper to Become a Pastor." The Gospel Coalition 14 Oct. 2009, 24 Aug. 2019 https://www.thegospelcoalition.org/blogs/Justin-Taylor/30-years-ago-today-how-god-called-john-piper-to-become-a-pastor/.
10. Harold J. Westing, *Church Staff Handbook* (Grand Rapids: Krefeld Publications, 1997) 172-173.
11. Banks, 23.
12. Vasile Filat, "Can you preach unprepared, only guided by the Holy Spirit?" Christian Moldova.md 28 Oct. 2017, 27 Aug. 2019 https://moldovacrestina.md/en/can-you-preach-unprepared-only-guided-by-the-holy-spirit/.
13. Exantus, 31.
14. Twenge, Jean M et al. "Generational and time period differences in American adolescents' religious orientation, 1966-2014." PloS one vol. 10,5 e0121454. 11 May. 2015, doi:10.1371/journal.pone.0121454.
15. Presser, Stanley, and Mike Chavez. "Is Religious Service Attendance Declining?" Journal for the Scientific Study of Religion, vol., 2007. https://onlinelibrary.wiley.com/doi/abs/10.1111/j.1468-

5906.2007.00367.x Accessed 9 Jan. 2020.
16 Jason K. Allen, "Eight Tips for Beginning Preachers," Jasonkallen.com 11 May 2016. 27 Aug. 2019 https://jasonkallen.com/2016/05/eight-tips-for-beginning-preachers/.
17 Paul Chappell, "Five Reasons Pastors Should Grow in Administrative Skills," Paulchappell.com 23 Apr 2018. 31 Aug. 2019 https://paulchappell.com/2018/04/23/five-reasons-pastors-should-grow-in-administrative-skills/.
18 Exantus, 70.
19 Banks, 5.

Chapter 3
MINISTERIAL EDUCATION, TRAINING AND MENTORSHIP

Just as the marketplace needs educated and trained staff, so does the church. Education and training develop individuals' knowledge, skills, and abilities. Education and training enhance one's strengths and modifies the weaknesses. God has birthed gifts and talents in all of His human creations. It is His plan to use them for the building of His church. The Apostle Paul said, *"The gifts He gave were that some would be apostles, some prophets, some evangelists, some pastors and teachers, to equip the saints for the work of ministry, and for the building up the body of Christ"* (Ephesians 4:11-12). A pastor must be able to teach (Titus 1:9; 1 Timothy 3:2) and must be spiritually mature (1 Timothy 3:6), which begins with and then grows through education, training, and mentorship.

We serve a God of order (1 Corinthians 1:14-33). Throughout Scripture, everyone who operated in their calling were taught, trained, and mentored. The Bible shows us that, when God has a person who is ready to lead, to commit to full discipleship, and to take on the responsibility for others, that person's calling is limitless. In the Scriptures, such leaders still had shortcomings and flaws, but despite those limitations, they served God as spiritual leaders.[1] God trained Adam how to till the land (Genesis 3:23). Moses mentored Joshua (Exodus 17:14; Exodus 33:11). Jethro mentored Moses (Exodus 18:17-24). Moses trained chosen men on how to judge the Israelites (Exodus 18:25-26). Jesus trained the disciples (Matthew 10:1; Matthew 11:1; Luke 11:1). Aquila and Priscilla taught Apollos (Acts 18:26).

Great is the desire to serve God and to declare love for all mankind, but if ill-equipped, the act of service may become overwhelming and burdensome. It can become grunt work, instead of a spiritually-rewarding assignment. When people and events do not flow as one envisioned, if not properly educated or trained, one may take offense and stop serving, questioning and resigning from the call. Blanchard and Hodges noted, "Do you know how long it took Jesus to change His disciples' attitudes and behaviors related to servant leadership? Three years of daily interaction."[2] Yet, the call to the ministry is typically a call for lifelong learning. Pastors become lifelong learners because their hearts desire knowledge and understanding and the calling requires it – lifelong learning is simply part of the job.

Lifelong learning is not just about learning and understanding the Scriptures. It is about learning how to serve and lead people. Working with people can be gratifying, and other times, disturbing. At times, it would be nice if ministry didn't entail people, but ministry is the act of serving people. It is the display of God's outstretched hand to all mankind. Imagine ministry as a full-service hospital. God has everything necessary to heal the needs of His people. In order to provide quality service, education and training are needed. An executive pastor said, "I have seen many pastors (friends) who stepped out to pastor the organism (church), but they are VERY frustrated with the leading of the organization." He stated that their common response is "I didn't know it would be this hard to work with church folks!" Rick Warren stated in *The Purpose-Driven Church*:

> Today the pastoral ministry is a hundred times more complex than it was just a generation ago. Even in the best circumstances, ministry is incredibly difficult. But there are also many more resources to help you if you avail yourself to them. The key is never stop learning.[3]

Awareness of Strengths and Weaknesses

Many ministers receive several accolades for their preaching and see people humbly responding to their altar calls, then they assume they have a pastoral call. It is not until they function as a pastor that reality sets in. With a focus on the pastoral education, training, and mentoring for ministers, Tom Rath stated, "Without an awareness of your strength, it's almost impossible for you to lead effectively."[4] Because awareness and self-assessments are subjective, it is also important and typically meaningful to enlist others in helping to more comprehensively assess those strengths and weaknesses.

Assessing strengths and weaknesses helps one reflect more deeply about the call to ministry. Rath added, "Although less noticeable, another serious problem occurs when people try to lead while having no clue about their natural strengths."[5] If one lacks self-confidence and temperance, the pastorate role is cumbersome. Everything would appear as an attack against one's character. One would view the church as an enemy. The church is supposed to show the world how to unconditionally love one another. Jesus said, *"By this shall all men know that ye are my disciples, if ye have love one to another"* (John 13:35). Hence, an awareness of weaknesses is not a means to the end of the pastoral journey; instead, it is a means to recognize ways to improve one's character, view of the church, and continue to nurture love for oneself and others.

This love does not mean there will not be disagreements or that tough times will not occur; but it does mean that God's people should not behave unlike Christ when conflict arises. It can be disheartening to see individuals serve in a leadership position and lack people-skills, but this may be a weakness. It can be embarrassing to the body of Christ when leadership does not know how to handle conflict, but that may be a weakness. One of the key lessons Jesus taught His disciples was about conflict: *"He who listens to you listens to me; he who rejects you rejects me: but he who rejects me rejects Him who sent me"* (Luke 10:16). We have to be reminded as pastors, if we are serving as unto the Lord (Colossians 3:23), the conflict is not with us but with God. Although the effects of the conflict may hurt or wound, we have to ask the Lord to help us not to view it as a personal attack. This is why education, training, and mentoring are crucial in ministry.

Educational Priorities

Recalling the 10 pastoral priorities listed in Chapter 2, there are knowledge, skills, and abilities needed to be learned and developed for an individual to efficiently operate in the pastoral role. For example, administrative duties mean the pastor needs to be an organizer. Matthew Branaugh from *Christianity Today* noted that, "Most church pastors state that church administration keeps them up at night. The list usually includes the management of finances, the liabilities of staff and volunteer misconduct, the handling of paperwork, tax compliance, and the upkeep of a facility."[6] Three top priorities for pastors in a contemporary society include prayer work, people work, and paperwork.

Counseling is a part of people work and means the pastor needs to be comfortable with problem solving. Oswald Sanders stated that one of the chief duties of leaders is to solve tough problems within the organization. Creating problems is easy; solving them is difficult. The leader must face the problem realistically, and follow through until the solution is reached.[7] Similarly, enabling duties means the pastor needs to be able to help the members identify their special call. Ken Davis claimed that a big part of a leader's role is to help equip others for the work of the ministry.[8] Equipping others to work for the ministry is just a part of people work.

With teaching and preaching, the pastor needs to be able to

rightly expound the Scriptures. Will Banks asked, "Do you delight in the study of God's Word, the Bible? Do you have the ability to communicate? Is there the 'fire shut up in your bones' conviction that you must preach?"[9] This delight, fire, and conviction must also be supported by prayer work.

However, as one can see, the call to the pastorate is more than a pulpit ministry. There is also paperwork. Because of the increased attention and interest in the concept of pastoral leadership in administration, scholars are beginning to examine its scale, necessity, and importance. For example, Sung Jun Kim isolated five key dimensions of pastoral administrative leadership (methods, processes, communication, culture, and structure) from sampling 1,000 full-time senior pastors who informed the researcher on these measures of pastoral administrative leadership.[10] The outcomes of such studies are indicators that administrative pastoral leadership is akin to educational leadership, potentially measurable, and can develop through broad exposure to education, training, and mentorship experiences.

Formal Education

Formal pastoral education is an ancient practice, with Catechetical schools providing basic Christian faith instruction, baptism, theological reflection, and ministerial training during the first centuries of the Christian movement. Later, monasteries became centers of theological academia then Protestant churches followed and founded seminaries specifically to train ministers, continuing as a significant resource in educating pastors for a leadership-oriented ministry.[11] At the start of the 21st century, there were over 200 top theological seminaries in the United States.[12]

The leadership structure of the majority of modern seminaries continue to be denominationally-based. The oldest seminary, which was established in 1816, is Harvard University Divinity School. The most recent was established in 2011, Bexley Seabury Seminary. Individuals who are interested in ministry and sense the need to be equipped for their calling have a tendency to question whether attending a Bible college or a seminary school would be most suitable.

According to research, Bible colleges are mostly associated with Protestant denominations. They offer bachelor's degrees, mostly in biblical studies, whereas, seminary is commonly associated with Catholicism and many other faiths. Theological seminaries offer instruction in Biblical studies, philosophy, leadership, and pastoral care courses. These can lead to bachelor's or master's degrees.[13] A former Vice-President of a community Bible college explained that there is an increase in pastors attending Bible institutions, trainings and seminars. He claimed, "Pastors, today, want to be better prepared in dealing with the multiplicity of issues that they face in the church."

In early 2000, when I sensed the call to ministry, I inquired about Biblical schooling, at which time, my husband was attending a local Bible college. Observing the wealth of knowledge he was gaining from each course, I decided to follow him and attend the college. We not only graduated from the college, but also we became employees. My husband served in administration for eleven years, and I was an adjunct professor for nine years.

In the past, Biblical knowledge was the only education needed for ministry, especially for the pastorate. James Berkley explained, "Today, there are educational and denominational requirements that precede ordination. Hebrew, Greek, preaching proficiency, all the tests and ordination exams—each becomes a major rite of passage."[14] A Director of Enrollment at a prominent theological seminary noted a decrease in clergy enrollment adding, "With more mainline denominations (such as Baptists and Pentecostals) requiring a Master of Divinity in order for one to be ordained, it has helped maintain enrollment in many seminaries." In addition, candidates for ordination in some mainline denominations (such as the Church of the Nazarene) typically complete at least three consecutive years of formal ministry before they are ordained, adding practical scenario-based experience to the development of pastors as leaders.

Informal Education

There are many forms of Biblical education, and not all training is formal. An example offered is that in many places throughout the world, people may be illiterate; yet, "Bible teaching in this context is still important, but may take a much different form than in a culture with a high level of formal education."[15] Scripture encourages Biblical education. *"Study to shew thyself approved unto God, a workman that needeth not to be ashamed, rightly dividing the word of truth"* (2 Timothy 2:15). In addition, experience contributes to pastors' development as church and spiritual leaders.

The questions arise: Does this rite of passage equip one for the pastorate? Does Bible college or seminary equip one to be an effective pastor for all the additional pastoral priorities previously mention? A female assistant pastor claimed that her 10-month ministerial internship program, church planters video conferencing, and annual leadership and development conferences equipped her to be an effective pastor. Following these informal educational and practical experiences, she and her husband shepherded two churches.

There are some who believe having the calling and God's anointing is more than enough as a pastor. Yet, Scriptures tell us to *"meditate in thy precepts, and have respect unto thy ways"* (Psalm 119:15). A female senior pastor stated that her Biblical foundation began in her church home, then she attended a Bible college that increased her Biblical knowledge. The Bible college professors were Spirit-filled and each class was a worship experience. She stated, "It was a totally different experience attending a prominent theological seminary." She added, "Seminaries provide so many theological perspectives and religions." Accordingly, one must be grounded in their faith in Jesus Christ, not easily persuaded to believe something else.

Not all pastors have the resources and time to receive pastoral education from a Bible college or seminary; and not having it doesn't negate the call of God on their lives. *"Thou shalt meditate therein day and night, that thou mayest observe to do according to all that is written therein: for then thou shalt make thy way prosperous, and then thou shalt have good success"* (Joshua 1:8). Church and denominational apprenticeships and trainings may be just as effective. In Andrew Hancock's doctoral research, he noted that seminaries are equipped to train students intellectually, but the local church best trains students through hands-on experience.[16]

In 2017, my husband and I attended a three-month leadership training sponsored by our denomination. The training was called LeaderLabs. It had 10 leadership tracks:

1. Integrity of the Heart
2. Self-Awareness
3. Leading Change
4. Servant Leadership
5. Leading Conflict
6. Situational Leadership
7. Water You Swim In
8. Transformational Leadership
9. The Road Ahead
10. Developing a Bench

This training exposed participants to fascinating leadership related concepts, theory and practical skills that are context sensitive to ministry and marketplace leaders.[17] This training transformed our leadership paradigm. We changed our leadership meeting formats from being logistical to coaching and empowerment. The team observed a complete difference in our method of relating to them. We were no longer task-focused and became more people-focused. We came to understand how an understanding of situational, transformational, and servant leadership styles have benefitted Christian leaders and followers in their commitments to lifelong learning and the church.

Situational Leadership

It has been argued that leadership is something that can be learned, improved, and taught to others. New learning models are opening up opportunities for Christian leadership understanding and growth. Christian leadership development programs and education curriculum are expanding each year, with the knowledge of how leadership theory and development benefit pastors, their followership, and the church. Situational leadership is one theory applied in Christian contexts to help leaders define and fill what followers need. These leaders do not treat all followers the same ways, nor do they lead and respond to any given single follower the same way in all circumstances. A situational leader analyzes situations, identifies what each follower needs in specific situations, and then proceeds accordingly. Situational leadership theory encompasses an understanding of delegating, directing, coaching, and supporting behaviors and their impact on others.[18]

Jesus demonstrated situational leadership with His interactions with the 12 disciples. He instructed them when they needed information, knowledge, or correction. He directed and redirected them when they were confused. He encouraged them when they were reluctant. And, He uplifted them when they were downhearted. At the right times and in the right places, He assigned progressively more significant tasks and responsibilities alongside Him, while guiding and supporting them. Ultimately, He empowered them. Through these actions, Jesus showed us that effective leadership can be situational and helps address what followers need.

Similarly, the Apostle Paul's ministry was driven to bring as many people as he could to embrace faith in Christ. He did so through a situational approach to leadership. For example, Paul said, *"I have become all things to all people so that by all possible means I might save some"* (1 Corinthians 9:22). He approached his tasks differently, depending on the followers and what he needed to do to reach, embolden, and empower them. In Colossians 4:5-6, Paul said, *"Be wise in the way you act toward outsiders, make the most of every opportunity. Let your conversation always be full of grace, seasoned with salt, so that you may know how to answer everyone."* For Paul, consciously and intentionally adapting his approach to each situation and person he confronted was the demonstration of situational leadership.

Pastors confront many different people in varied contexts. They depend often on volunteers and on a diverse body of church members to help build and grow the church and to minister effectively to people from all walks of life with many different needs. Accordingly, the pastor must be able to embrace and demonstrate appropriate flexibility of leadership style, as did Jesus and Paul, in the tasks, roles, and responsibilities of church leadership. An understanding of these leadership concepts and theories, through meaningful education, study, and reflection, enables pastors to appreciate how their actions and behaviors can more optimally influence and support others and the church. Situational leadership is not exclusive of the other forms of leadership styles, so an appreciation of leadership theory through learning and practiced applications can help pastors and their membership grow through Christ.

Servant Leadership

The growing body of leadership research tells us that there is an enhanced understanding of the concept in the marketplace and in conventional theory. However, in seminary and theology schools, servant leadership has slowly become a core course for pastoral and lay ministry. The interesting fact is that Jesus Christ Himself provided the best example of servant leadership throughout His life here on earth. In Scriptures, one reads how Jesus humbled Himself and washed the feet of His disciples, found in John 13:3-5:

> *"Jesus, knowing that the Father had given all things into His hands, and that He had come from God and was going to God, rose from supper and laid aside His garments, took a towel and girded himself. After that, He poured water into a basin and began to wash the disciples' feet, and to wipe them with the towel with which He was girded."*

After performing a servant duty, He explained His actions to encourage His team of leaders to do likewise:

> *"So when He had washed their feet, taken His garments, and sat down again, He said to them, "Do you know what I have done to you? You call me Teacher and Lord, and you say well, for so I am. If I then, your Lord and Teacher, have washed your feet, you also ought to wash one another's feet. For I have given you an example, that you should do as I have done to you. Most assuredly, I say to you, a servant is not greater than*

His master; nor is He who is sent greater than He who sent him. If you know these things, blessed are you if you do them" (John 13:12-17).

As servant-leaders, the blessing is working alongside your staff to fulfill organizational goals, not only meeting goals, but also establishing relationships that usually do not occur in controlled leadership. There are benefits of servant leadership that aids pastoral ministry. The example Jesus displayed in John 13 is the kind of servant leadership that produces a church filled with real purpose and motivation as people are called, appreciated, loved, encouraged disciples, involved by mentoring and discipleship before they are deployed in ministry.[19]

As a servant-leader, one purposefully sets aside judgments and presuppositions about staff and intentionally establishes opportunities to become acquainted with each team member. In companion sessions, one learns each individual's strengths and weakness, their prejudices and passions, and successes and failures. The marketplace identifies this practice as Leadership Coaching. Instead of the leader giving instructions on how to perform a job, the leader empowers each individual on the team to create their own performance plan according to their characteristics and skills. As a servant-leader, one learns to depend on the ideas of the team.

Servant-leaders are not afraid to take ownership of personal deficits or misfortunes in the ministry. Instead of placing the blame on an individual or others, the servant-leader learns to assess the problem and work with the team members to determine a better method. John Pellowe stated, "Servant leadership is not just about doing, it is also about a way of thinking. It is about recognizing a higher authority than one's self, and acknowledging that the goal of leadership is to benefit others."[20] The benefit is all parties understand that "we all are in this together."

The old adage, "Change is good" still holds true today. Servant-leaders understand that anything that remains the same can become stagnate and ineffective. Christ is not a stagnant and ineffective God. He brought forth change when He entered Mary's womb, because she was a virgin. It was outside of the norm and human nature. This change led to hope, deliverance, and salvation to a dying world. Although God does not change (Malachi 3:6), He causes change. Throughout Scripture, one sees God shifting seasons, nature, characters, and people's plans to fulfill His purpose. Therefore servant-leaders learn not to fight change, but to flow with the wave current. However, change management is not a concept that can be understood without adequate appreciation for how to best go about the process, which is a part of what can be honed through formal leadership training.

Quite often, leaders are visionaries. They see the larger picture, but they lack the creativity and perception to manifest the vision. A servant-leader is not ashamed or embarrassed to present the vision to the team and solicit their ideas. This is a sign of humility and people appreciate the opportunity to partner with a leader who isn't seeking self-notoriety. Yet, for some, these approaches in leadership style do not emerge naturally. Hence, leadership training is a purposeful and meaningful approach to strengthening one's preparation to more fully serve the church.

Transformational Leadership

Although ministry is revolved around one person, Jesus Christ, the methods and approaches to serving are ever-changing. God never commanded His pastors to serve as dictators nor as loners. Jesus and the disciples lived and feasted together before He died. He informed the disciples that He would never leave them alone and comfortless and promised they would have the Holy Spirit to always lead and guide them into all truth (John 14:16-18, 26). Transformational leaders seek multiple ways to serve God and His people. For pastors to maintain sanctity of mind and heart, they need to assess their leadership styles.

Throughout Jesus' three-year ministry, He functioned as both a servant and a transformational leader. The only times when Jesus was alone was during His private time of prayer with the Heavenly Father. The majority of His leadership time was spent teaching and equipping the disciples to serve and to transform. Like servant leadership concepts, transformational leadership theory also made a significant impact across all levels of leadership practices, including Christianity. The tenets of transformational leadership theory are becoming a growing mainstay of many formal and informal educational programs.

The emphasis of transformational leadership theory is on self-reflection and motivating people to transcend self-interests. Jesus was the great example of servant leadership who also transformed the lives of others and of worship. As with servant leadership, transformational leadership develops unity in the church. The pastor establishes a clear understanding that they all must work together to build the kingdom of God. There are no big i's and little t's in fulfilling God's ultimate plan of salvation. Pastors who are transformational leaders are aware that they cannot reach their designated community alone. In *Simple Church,* Thom Rainer and Eric Geiger stated, "God desires the miracle of unity for the church…Without the miracle of unity, churches divide and ministry suffers. And all of this occurs while the world watches."[21] Transformational leadership facilitates deeper communication between the leader and follower, as leaders holistically engage followers to grow collectively in the achievement of organizational and spiritual goals.

The transformational leader also helps shape the view of the church. Sadly, in the 21st century, the world has seen church and denominational wars, from a difference in theological opinions to the battle of possession of church property. Andy Salgado wrote, "Unfortunately, wars, divisions, and church splits, have made the church look bad in the eyes of believers and unbelievers alike."[22] People may withdraw from the church with the belief that others are hypocrites, gossipers, and are fighting with each other. When a pastor establishes a transformational leadership mentality, they embrace their role as a steward over the things God has entrusted and when one embraces this attitude, it will help the individual not to feel so overwhelmed in their obligation to transform others through their pastoral leadership. Jesus was transformational in the ways He inspired others to follow Him and to share the gospel. He established unique relationships with each person and demonstrated mentorship while also encouraging other disciples and believers to be mentors.

Pastoral Mentorship

Mentorship is another asset to educating and training individuals for the pastorate. Mentoring provides a more personal and intimate experience with those who are leading and being led. One may see first-hand experiences of the pastorate. Mentoring can be an ongoing, beneficial activity as long as one is open to someone speaking into their life.[23] Mentorship can be time-consuming, but it requires more of a commitment from both parties. Both individuals must commit to availability, honesty, and respect towards one another. In doing so, it is possible to build belief in oneself and help replace followers' fears and doubts with a sense of value and vision, as explained by Roger Elrod:

Although some followers can believe in the value of a

leader's vision, they may not believe they're good enough or spiritual enough to fulfill it. They doubt themselves more than they doubt their pastor's leadership. So, our leading and feeding will be to no avail unless we believe in our people.[24]

A Biblical example of pastoral mentorship is the Apostle Paul and Timothy, the pastor of the Crete churches. Paul's letters to Timothy were written as a spiritual father to a spiritual son. *"Timothy, guard what has been entrusted to your care. Turn away from godless chatter and the opposing ideas of what is falsely called knowledge"* (1 Timothy 6:20). *"Preach the word; be prepared in season and out of season; correct, rebuke and encourage—with great patience and careful instruction"* (2 Timothy 4:2). "Furthermore:

> *"What you heard from me, keep as the pattern of sound teaching, with faith and love in Christ Jesus. Guard the good deposit that was entrusted to you—guard it with the help of the Holy Spirit who lives in us"* (2 Timothy 1:13-14).

About mentoring, one female pastor said, "Pastoring can be challenging and draining, but knowing there are others who have traveled the same path. Learning from them and their experiences can be reassuring and encouraging." Another pastor claimed that one's experience and guidance of others may help new pastors with overcoming similar situations and frustrations.

From my peer research, the resounding statement amongst ministers, pastors, and Christian educators is oriented toward "Pastoral Mentorship." They all believed that it would be more positively influential for new pastors than education and training. Mentorship would provide upfront, current, and relevant experiences with today's congregants and church administration.

Mentorship will channel the individual beyond the mindset that pastoring is only preaching, teaching, officiating wedding and funerals, and making hospital visits.

In closing, ministerial education, training, and mentoring are aids for equipping individuals to become better servants of God. As one Christian educator explained, "Pastors must be life-long learners. If God is infinite, then one's life must be spent ever-searching, ever-questioning, and ever-pressing to know God's revelation about himself and eternity." In the midst of all this necessary biblical knowledge and experience, pastors are trying to balance life, family, and the church's expectations daily. Chapter 4 will address pastors having to overcome and balance self, family, church, and societal expectations.

Endnotes

1. J. Oswald Sanders, *Spiritual Leadership*, (Chicago: Moody Publishers, 2007) 17.
2. Ken Blanchard and Phil Hodges, *Lead Like Jesus*, (Nashville: Thomas Nelson, 2005) xii.
3. Rick Warren, *The Purpose-Driven Church*, (Grand Rapids: Zondervan, 1995) 20.
4. Tom Rath, *Strengths Based Leadership*, (New York: Gallup Press, 2008) 10.
5. Ibid. 11.
6. Matthew Branaugh, "5 Church Administration Issues You Need to Know—But Didn't Learn in Seminary," *Christianity Today* 9 Jul. 2016, 3 Sept. 2019 https://www.christianitytoday.com/pastors/2016/July-web-exclusive-church-administration-issues-you-need-to-know-but-didn't-I.html.
7. Sanders, 113.
8. Ken Davis, *7 Keys to Lead Successful House Groups*, (Middletown: Elevitamedia, 2015) 69.
9. William L. Banks, *Pastor's Pal* (Fort Washington: CLC Publications, 2007) 5
10. Sung Joong Kim, "Development of Pastoral Administrative Leadership Scale Based on the Theories of Educational Leadership," Jan. 9, 2020. https://www.tandfonline.com/doi/full/10.1080/23311975.2019.1579963
11. Hayes, Justin L., "An Analysis of Education and Experience in Pastoral Leadership Development" (2015). Ed.D. Books. 78. https://digitalcommons.olivet.edu/edd_diss/78
12. Top Theological Seminaries," *Church Relevance,* 10 Sept. 2019 https://churchrelevance.com/resources/theological-seminaries-list/.
13. "Difference between Bible College and Seminary," difference.guru, 10 Sept. 2019 https://www.google.com/amp/s/difference.guru/difference-between-bible-college-and-seminary/amp/.
14. James D. Berkley, General Editor, *Leadership Handbook of Management and Administration* (Grand Rapids: Baker Books, 16-17) 1994
15. Is a formal Bible education necessary for a pastor?" *Christian Truth,* 10 Sept. 2019 https://www.compellingtruth.org/pastor-education.html.
16. Andrew Hancock, "Pastoral Training in the Local Church,"

Amicalled.com, 15 Mar. 2018, 16 Sept. 2019 https://amicable.com/2018/03/pastoral-training-local-church/.

17 LeaderLabs, 16 Sept. 2019 https://www.leaderlabs.com/what-is-the-10es-elp.
18 Belet, Daniel. (2016). "Enhancing Leadership Skills with Action Learning." *Development and Learning in Organizations: An International Journal,* 2016, 30, 13-15. doi:10.1108/DLO-06-2016-0049.
19 Servant Leadership," Institute of Church Leadership Development, 11 Jan. 2020 http:///www.churchleadership.org/68920.
20 John Pellowe, "Servant leaders: Whom do they serve?" *Canadian Council of Christian Charities,* 22 Apr. 2013, 11 Jan. 2020 https://www.ccc.org/news_blogs/john/2013/04/22/servant-leaders-whom-do-they-serve/.
21 Thom S. Rainer and Eric Geiger, *Simple Church* (Nashville: B&H Publishing Group, 2011) 167.
22 Andy Salgado, "Denominations: Have They Brought Civil War Within the Church?" *Medium,* 22 Oct. 2017, 11 Jan. 2020 https://medium.com/christian-perspectives-society-and-life/denominations-have-they-brought-civil-war-within-the-church-5fa6b8e6dc1a.
23 "Why Pastors Need Mentors and How to Find One," Church Fuel, 27 Feb. 2019, 16 Sept. 19 https://churchleaders.com/pastors/pastor-articles/345232-why-pastors-need-a-mentor-and-how-to-find-one.html.
24 Berkley, 177-78.

Rise and Fall of Pastors in the 21st Century

Chapter 4
EXPECTATIONS

In any relationship, each individual or party begins with expectations. One may have higher expectations than the other. Both may have equal expectations.[1] Whatever the circumstance may be, each one desires something. *Webster* defines expectation as something anticipated, and a looking forward with hope or pleasure. When one receives Jesus as Savior, she or he is hoping for a life better than the present one. The sermon message heard, the song sung, or the act of compassion shown by a Christian believer caused an individual to respond to Christ's invitation to salvation. Now the individual is a Christian—one who has a relationship with Jesus Christ.

Like any relationship, there are several forms of anticipation: self-fulfillment, self-gratification, self-denial, self-admiration, and self-respect. I listed a few to give a general understanding, but the list is endless. Kenneth Gangel described the church as an organism—the body of Christ—living, changing, and supernatural in its very being. He further noted that the church is also an organization that functions as a group of people who operate according to bylaws, objectives, officers, and budgets.[2]

Everyone who attends a church service is not assumed to be a Christian, but everyone who chooses to be a member of a church is assumed to be a Christian. A member is one who has agreed and accepted the teachings, doctrines, and governance of a church. Some churches may have a formal method of establishing church and members' relationships or partnerships. Overall, in this agreement, there are expectations from both parties. In this chapter, there is an exploration of Scriptural and researched expectations which, in the end, will lead to a discussion of the expectations of pastors, church leaders, and church members in the 21st century.

Scriptural Expectations

The Hebrew meaning for expectation in Psalm is an attachment (like a cord), a hope, and a longing for.[3] *"My soul, wait thou only upon God; for my expectation is from him"* (Psalm 62:5). There are two Greek meanings for expectation. In Luke, it means to watch and to anticipate in thought, hope, or fear. *"And as the people were in expectation, and all men mused in their hearts of John, whether he were the Christ, or not"* (Luke 3:15). The other meaning in Philippians is to have an intense anticipation.[4] *"According to my earnest expectation and my hope, that in nothing I shall be ashamed, but that with all boldness, as always, so now also Christ shall be magnified in my body, whether it be by life, or by death"* (Philippians 1:20). In all three contexts, the expectation is in God, not in man. I believe if one channels expectations and anticipations in the appropriate One, God Himself, it may aid in not being so easily disappointed or offended.

Referring back to Chapter 1, God's intent for pastors is to feed and lead His sheep to Him. Anything that deviates from God's intention may be a distraction or hindrance to God's ultimate plan. The Apostle Paul encourages the sheep (those who are followers of the shepherd) to pray for them: *"Brethren pray for us"* (1 Thessalonians 5:25). Paul said:

> *"I exhort therefore, that, first of all, supplications, prayers, intercessions, and giving of thanks, be made for all men; for kings, and for all that are in authority; that we may lead a quiet and peaceable life in all godliness and honesty"*
> (1 Timothy 2:1-2).

The Expectations

When one intercedes for another, it is a matter of the heart and the internal work of the Holy Spirit. It is difficult to be easily irritated or to remain angry with that individual. Bearing this Scriptural insight, pastoral and membership expectations have a tendency to cause a burden to ministry.

Servant-leaders practice behavior management. They know that there will be times of chaos, misunderstandings, and misinterpretations, but they must remain their composure. Pastoral servant-leaders must learn from Scriptures. The Bible provides several examples of leaders who were loose-cannons and those who were temperament. The temperament response most of the times produced favorable results.

In *Healthy Churches,* David Keck said, "Our expectations powerfully shape our interactions with others. They shape how we perceive, how we experience, and how we respond."[5] Most pastors enter a church anticipating to make a significant impact in the lives of the parishioners and the community. There is hope for a team-spirit with the leadership, love, and compassion amongst the membership, and a plan of unity to destroy the works of evil. At times, this may be a pastor's picturesque idea of ministry. The reality is that a pastor may enter a church with disgruntled leadership and membership, little or no financial income to fulfill ministry needs, and unstable residence for family. Douglas Rumford summed up pastoral expectations:

> As pastors, our search for a ministry position is much more than a job hunt; it is the search for the place where we can fruitfully exercise our gifts in and through the Christian community. It is a process that touches every dimension of our lives—personal, family, and vocational—as well as the present and future congregations.[6]

Rise and Fall of Pastors in the 21st Century

High Hopes

I interviewed four Protestant pastors to gain a 21st century perspective of their expectations of the church. This pastoral poll consisted of three males and one female pastor. Their pastoral tenure ranged from five to twenty years. All four pastors' church membership consisted of Centennials to Traditionalists. Their average worship service attendance ranged between 20 and 300. The three male pastors' churches were in a suburban community. The female pastor's church was in an urban community.

The consensus amongst these pastors was that of high hopes for their congregations. One male pastor had been in ministry for over forty years and planted a church five years ago. He continues to have high hopes for his congregation, and they are aware of it. He also expresses God's high hopes for them to fulfill their God-given purpose. The female pastor stated, "I express not only my high hopes to the congregation, but I have been impressing upon them the flavor of the world and the intensity of ministry during this season." She encourages her congregation to do ministry outside of the four walls of the church. Another male pastor who is shepherding his second church, within his five-year tenure, stated that his hope is that the church members will be influential, engaged, and significant individuals within their social circles. He said, "I believe that each member of my congregation will be influential and blessed as each one focuses on the Lord's call to live our lives with love, obedience, and service." Pastoral hope is a starting point for the construction and framing of expectations.

The responding pastors rated their expectation levels for their churches, with the average being mid-scale. The most frequent idea expressed was that expectations in relationships are formed on a case-by-case basis. Regarding membership, rather than expectations, the common focus amongst the pastors was their hopes in keeping

The Expectations

the congregation engaged in serving God. The female pastor said, "We expect a lot from God, but God also expects a lot from us." Scriptural reference to this hope and expectation also address unity and the calling:

> *"I therefore, a prisoner for the Lord, urge you to walk in a manner worthy of the calling to which you have been called, with all humility and gentleness, with patience, bearing with one another in love, eager to maintain the unity of the Spirit in the bond of peace. There is one body and one Spirit—just as you were called to the one hope that belongs to your call— one Lord, one faith, one baptism, one God and Father of all, who is over all and through all and in all"* (Ephesians 4:1-6).

Member Expectations

Jesus warned those who wanted to follow Him and be His disciple: *"The foxes have holes, and the birds of the air have nests; but the Son of man have no where to lay His head"* (Matthew 8:20). He was informing them that life in the natural was not comfortable, nor was it convenient. There will always be times of sacrifice and uncertainties. Therefore, servants of Christ must be reminded that, although their expectations may not always be met, they must continue to serve in spite of it. Keck noted that many of the most common difficulties in churches arise from congregation members and their leaders (pastors) failing to discuss priorities and expectations and not finding ways to work through the problems that arise when expectations are not met.[7]

I interviewed four members of Protestant churches: two females and two males. Three were residents of Maryland and one resided in Southern Virginia. Their ages ranged from 25 to 55. They all were active church members and answered questions about three things they expect from their pastors. One of the female respondents stated that she expected weekly Bible study, prayer when needed, and hospital visitations. A male respondent replied, "I expect Scriptural understanding, an ability to listen, and a teaching ability." A common response from all four church members was that the pastor must be one who is Spirit-led, able to teach Scriptures, and have a heart for people (no favoritism). In response to whether their pastors met those expectations, all respondents described their pastors as one who works alongside the members and freely interacts with them. One respondent stated that his pastor maintains an air of humility and friendliness that crosses various barriers for most.

I asked all four church members if they thought their expectations of their pastors were realistic or fair. One female respondent believed her expectations were fair. She stated, "My pastor conducts Bible Study every Wednesday night. He never fails to pray for me when I need it, and hospital visitations are a part of his ministry." One male respondent believed his expectations were realistic. He claimed, "A pastor should be committed to a personal holiness and having a relationship with God." The expectations for pastoral leadership are varied and may be even seem daunting, but the expectations of the members are also juxtaposed with the expectations or self-image of good pastoral leadership that pastors may hold, leads to more complicated and challenging scenarios.

For example, I presented the same questions to the pastors. The consistent expectations included a pastor who is knowledgeable about Scriptures and is able to teach it, one whose life exemplifies Christ, and one who is available to talk and counsel. There was a divide in viewing these expectations as fair or realistic. While the majority of pastors agreed that most expectations were realistic and reasonable, one pastor commented that members may maintain unrealistic expectations, such as pastors having the "answer to life's difficulties, hardships and heart breaks …to be available, present, and engaged in a moment's notice… regardless of the time of day or night." Another unrealistic expectation was "to be perfect…under the microscope of everyone's expectations of what a pastor should look like, sound like, or act like." One pastor said, "I believe that we have to take each expectation on a case-by-case basis." Yet, when looking at expectations on a case-by-case basis, one might become overwhelmed with the magnitude of responsibility. Servant-leaders understand from Scripture that Jesus approached people differently when presenting the gospel. The Apostle Paul had to be flexible to reach all cultures. He stated:

> *"For though I am free from all men, I have made myself a servant to all, that I might win the more; and to the Jews I became as a Jew, that I might win Jews; to those who are under the law, as under the law, that I might win those who are under the law; to those who are without law, as without law (not being without law toward God, but under law toward Christ), that I might win those who are without law; to the weak I became as weak, that I might win the weak. I have become all things to all men, that I might by all means save some"* (1 Corinthians 9:19-22).

These considerations and findings support possible explanations for results of surveys of pastors and their spouses. For example, a 2018 pastoral survey revealed that 54% found pastoring to be overwhelming and 80% felt unqualified and discouraged.[8] The same ministry survey revealed that 52% pastors feel overworked and felt unable to meet their church's unrealistic expectations. Eighty percent of pastors expect conflict within their church. Twenty-two percent of pastors' spouses felt that the ministry places undue expectations on their families.[9]

Rise and Fall of Pastors in the 21st Century

In Paul Tripp's book, *Dangerous Calling*, he lists some unrealistic expectations that most churches have of pastors: These include the idea that pastors should not "struggle with sin…[or] be tempted toward bitterness or envy…should be model spouses/parents… content with less pay than most with the same level of education… [and] should not face fears in meetings, the pulpit, and when dealing with people."[10] These are unrealistic expectations of any human being, but some pastors have these same assumptions about themselves, which can be a cause of increase pastoral burnout.

Recently, I attended a ministers and spouses' soul Sabbath get-a-way. It was a two-and-a-half-day retreat in Ocean City, Maryland. The vision of the Regional Administrative Bishop and facilitator was to replenish God's servants and to provide a unique, holistic experience in soul care. In one of the sessions, there was a PowerPoint slide titled, "Ministry is a Dangerous Career." Discussed was the recent landmark research which linked the following factors to spikes in ministerial burnout and career dissatisfaction among Assemblies of God ministers: (a) lack of control, (b) unclear job expectations, and (c) dysfunctional workplace dynamics.[11] We can again return to Scriptural guidance: *"Shepherd the flock of God among you, exercising oversight, not under compulsion, but willingly, as God would have you; not for shameful gain, but eagerly; not domineering over those in your charge, but being examples to the flock "*(1 Peter 5:2-3). It follows that pastors must be willing, but not compulsive, eager but not shameful, and controlled but not domineering.

Reconciling Expectations

As a result of the highlighted issues, pastors and their congregations struggle with reconciling unrealistic expectations for pastoral leadership. The promotion of unrealistic expectations from others are likely to foster internal unrealistic pastoral expectations, continued by their inherent need to achieve and succeed. Reconciling unrealistic expectations can involve an active process of building awareness of potential or real problems that can surface, and purposefully building realistic expectations. Church conflicts and divisions usually stem from lack of communication, an assumption of character, and differences of opinions and perspectives. Scripture addresses each of these issues. From Romans, we are told:

> *"For I say, through the grace given unto me, to every man that is among you, not to think of himself more highly than he ought to think; but to think soberly, according as God hath dealt to every man the measure of faith"* (Romans 12:3).

From Matthew, we are taught:

> *"Therefore if thou bring a gift to the altar, and there remember that thy brother hath ought against thee; leave there the gift before the altar, and go thy way; first be reconciled to thy brother, and then come and offer thy gift"* (Matthew 5:23-24).

We are also told that, *"By this shall all men know that ye are my disciples, if ye have love one to another"* (John 13:35). As Christians, we understand that no one is perfect, except Christ. Daily, we ought to mature to become more Christ-like. Identifying with Christ entails balancing our own expectations and working together to fulfill the purpose and plans of God.

Reconciling is the process of restoration or reestablishing health balance in relationships. For Christians, the restoration of friendly relations is a demonstration of the love, peace, and unity that we have in Jesus Christ. Reconciliation is the fulfillment of what Jesus directed us to do, which is to love one another (John 13:34-35; John 15:12). Yet, weaknesses such as ambition or seeking personal rewards can undermine the commitment to restorative relationships, making humankind susceptible to the battle. Balancing those expectations demonstrates that relationships are more important than both the concept of self and of religion, although the self, the relationship, and religion are ingredients necessary for Christian leadership to succeed. In an effort to reconcile the potential conflicts, Oswald Sanders listed the natural battles that common leaders face regularly. He balanced each battle with a spiritual characteristic that needs to be developed to serve as a successful leader. I called them "Leadership Expectation Battles" as shown in Table 1:[12]

Table 1
Leadership Expectation Battles

Natural	Spiritual
Self-confident	Confident in God
Knows men	Also Knows God
Makes own decisions	Seeks God's will
Ambitious	Humble
Creates methods	Follows God's example
Enjoys command	Delights in obedience to God
Seeks personal reward	Loves God and others
Independent	Depends on God

These natural characteristics are usually seen in many of the prominent and successful leaders that we observe in political and marketplace leaders. Many would conclude that these characteristics are the reasons for their business success and other notable accomplishments. These same natural traits may be developed innately in today's pastors; therefore, they struggle with the spiritual traits to become the shepherds that God has called them to be. The pastor does carry the burden of ministry and the church, but is not expected to bear it solely. God never intended the work of ministry to be a solo assignment. The Apostle Paul encouraged the body (church) to work together, grow, and build one another as each one does his part in ministry (Ephesians 4:16). Believers share in the Holy Spirit who empowers them to humbly seek the will of God. The more time spent in God's Word, the more the Holy Spirit transforms the mind to think like Christ. Reconciliation therefore becomes easier when seeking the lead of the Holy Spirit.

Expectations as Servant-Leaders

Servant-leaders function well in structure and may adapt to disorder to fulfill a mission. Servant-leaders practiced organizational skills before they were appointed to leadership, because they understand that they must dedicate themselves and their leadership to the organization's mission.[13] The servant-leader's calling to serve requires an ability to listen and perceive the needs of others. Servant-leaders create space for individual voices to grow and be heard. Robert E. Greenleaf Center for Servant Leadership tells us that, "Servant leadership becomes a living and breathing way of life when we respect and value the act of listening that allows us to increase our knowledge base and be able to empathize with another point of view." The lives of servant-leaders grow when they tune into others and "share communication in a space of reciprocity."[14]

Working in the reverse, servant-leaders also call upon others to also serve. Many of the pastors I surveyed agreed that they were comfortable in asking for help from the leadership and congregation. One pastor stated that he believed it develops and enhances the church. Congregants often appreciate pastors who invite and encourage involvement in ministry. They sense a level of cohesion in the church. Another pastor stated to his church, "If I do not get help with ministries, as well as visitations and outreaches, then they will not take place." Keck said:

> Pastors are called to model their ministry after the example of Jesus, who came 'not to be served but to serve.' They follow the Good Shepherd who risks his life for the sheep. In their role as shepherds, pastors lead, but they do so for the sake of the flock under their care. Therefore they are called to be servant leaders.[15]

An expectation of servant-leaders is that they encourage and build other leaders. There is a common leadership quote that I asked the pastors: "Does your congregation exhibit the 80-20 phenomenon—20 percent of the people do 80 percent of the work?" One of the male pastors stated that their church has exceeded such expectations and achieved a new phenomenon. He said, "Thirty-percent of the congregation does most of the work, because they are coached and mentored by me and other leaders. This hands-on approach triggers a positive reinforcement that rewards most who are active in the ministry." The female pastor believed this phenomenon is true in any congregation. She described, "a core of people do most of the work…the only way you can change this is to impress upon them that they need to get involved. We need to encompass those and encourage them to participate in ministry." Another male pastor stated that it is not true for his ministry because they are fairly new. He said, "I encourage them to understand that we need everyone to participate in building the Kingdom of God together by using their talents and gifts that the Lord has given unto them." Raising up leaders in the church requires encouragement.

I also interviewed two leaders who serve in the same church (one female and one male). I asked: Does your pastor seem more like a servant, leader, or a servant-leader? Both agreed that their pastor is a servant leader. The male leader stated, "Many members of the congregation have seen Pastor picking up trash, cleaning the bathrooms, and shoveling snow on the church parking lot." The female respondent noted that the pastor is not only involved with the congregation, but he also does community outreach. He facilitates evangelism training and mentors other pastors and ministers. Keck noted, "Healthy congregations thrive because their pastors consistently keep everyone's attention on Christ. Faithful pastors thrive because their congregation are focused on God."[16] The key to pastors maintaining a proper balance in ministry and keeping people on task, is redirecting their attention back to the Good Shepherd, Jesus Christ (John 10:14).

As we reflect on servant leadership in the 21st century, we recognize that there are some pastors who are demanding to be served instead of embracing Jesus' example of servanthood. Some have taken Proverbs 3:27 out of context, which says, *"Do not withhold good from those to whom it is due, when it is in your power to act."* At any moment, one might hear a pastor say, "People are to give honor where honor is due." Therefore, they have concluded that church members serving them is an act of honor. Throughout Scripture, Jesus was very direct in the importance of servanthood as he explained, *"The greatest among you will be your servant"* (Matthew 23:11). Jesus also said, *"Very truly I tell you, no servant is greater than his master, nor is a messenger greater than the one who sent Him"* (John 13:16). Furthermore, Jesus directed us to, *"Worship the Lord your God and serve Him only"* (Luke 4:8).

As simple as the concept of service may seem, Jayson Bradley stated, "A pastor's relationship with the church is complex. Negotiating the various expectations that individuals place on pastors can be tough, especially when they seem arbitrary or mutually exclusive."[17] He concluded in his 10-point research that church members are seeking shepherds who spend time with God, study, and are able to expound on the Scriptures, being self-aware, and working toward the vision for the church. Conversely, John McKeever researched the expectations of every congregation and stated, "In a very real sense, believers who support the work of the Lord with their tithes and offerings and time and energy have a right to expect certain things from their shepherd. That's what this is about."[18] It is possible that such thinking contributes to some pastors feeling overwhelmed and burnt out in ministry.

As noted in Chapter 3, many pastors stated that seminary education did not prepare them for the demands of the church. They agreed that it prepared them to rightly explain the word of God, but it did not equip them to meet the personal expectations of the church members. As a seminary professor, Paul Tripp stated that he wanted his students to understand they were called not just to preach exegetically correct and theologically precise sermons but also to pastor people, to walk, live, support, and suffer with them. He said, "I longed for them to understand that they aren't called just to teach theology to their people but also to do theology with their people."[19] Scriptures give us additional insight:

> *"Brothers, think of what you were when you were called. Not many of you were wise by human standards; not many were influential; not many were of noble birth. But God chose the foolish things of the world to shame the wise; God chose the weak things of the world to shame the strong"* (1 Corinthians 1: 26-27).

The Expectations

In closing, it is not incorrect or inappropriate to have expectations in the church. Expectations shape relationships. Expectations become a burden when pastors embrace an image that God has not ordained. Usually, this image leads to an assumption that church members seek an invincible shepherd, instead of one who will walk alongside them, teach them the Biblical truths, and love them unconditionally. As Keck emphasized, "Faithful pastors and healthy churches must agree to communicate covenant expectations in order to thrive together."

Endnotes

1. *The New Webster's Comprehensive Dictionary of the English Language, Deluxe Edition* (New York: American International Press, 1990) 332.
2. Kenneth O. Gangel, *Feeding & Leading* (Grand Rapids, Baker Books, 1989) 57-58.
3. James Strong, LL.D., S.T.D., *The New Strong's Exhaustive Concordance of the Bible* (Nashville: Thomas Nelson Publishers, 1990) 154
4. Ibid, 76.
5. David Keck, *Healthy Churches, Faithful Pastors* (London: Rowman & Littlefield, 2014) 11.
6. James D. Berkley, General Editor, *Leadership Handbook of Management and Administration* (Grand Rapids: Baker Books, 1994) 113.
7. Keck, 1.
8. "A Solutions-Focused Ministry," *Pastoral Care, Inc.*, 17 Sept. 19 https://www.pastoralcareinc.com.
9. "Statistics in the Ministry," *Ministry Missing Link*, 4 Oct. 2019 https://www.pastotalcareinc.com/statistics/.
10. Paul David Tripp, *Dangerous Calling* (Wheaton: Crossway, 2012) 93.
11. "Ministry-Related Burnout and Stress Coping Mechanisms Among Assemblies of God-Ordained Clergy in Minnesota," Research Gate, Aug. 2016, 12 Oct. 2019 https://www.researchgate.net/publications_Among_Assemblies_of_God_Clergy_in_Minnesota/amp.
12. J. Oswald Sanders, *Spiritual Leadership* (Chicago: Moody Publishers, 2007) 29.
13. Ibid, 2.
14. Robert E. Greenleaf Center for Servant Leadership. 6 Jan. 2020 https://www.greenleaf.org/listen-to-serve-servant-leadership-and-the-practice-of-effective-listening/
15. Keck, 81.
16. Ibid, 47.
17. Jayson D. Bradley, "10 Qualities Church Members Expect in a Pastor," *Ministry Advice*, 4 Jan. 2017, 17 Sept. 2019 https://ministryadvice.com/pastoral-expectations/.
18. Joe McKeever, "7 Expectations Every Congregation Should Have

for Their Pastor," Crosswalk, 30 Nov. 2016, 17 Sept. 19 https://www.crosswalk.com/blogs/joe-mckeever/7-expectations-every-congregation-should-have-for-their-pastor.html.

19 Tripp, 43.

Rise and Fall of Pastors in the 21st Century

Chapter 5
THE PASTOR'S FAMILY

Ministry is not only performed in the church; it also takes place in the home. It has been said, "One's first ministry is his family; everything else follows." Although ministry is an individual call by God, it does involve the minister's family. The biblical definition of minister and ministry is one who serves another.[1] Therefore, a minister must establish a proper balance in serving his family, his church, and his community.

Healthiness of Families

Pastors must manage stress and pressures from the multitude of demands, which can negatively impact them, their family members, and constituencies. According to a 2007 survey by *Leadership* magazine, ministers and their spouses responded that they have problems in the following areas:[2]

81 %	Insufficient time together	53 %	Raising children
71 %	Use of money	46 %	Sexual problems
70 %	Income level	41 %	Pastor's anger toward the spouse
64 %	Communication problems	35 %	Differences over ministry career
57 %	Differences over leisure	24 %	Differences over spouse's career

Eleven years later, a similar survey was conducted by *Pastoralcareinc.com* which revealed how ministry was related to the following problems among pastors' families:[3]

90 %	Ministry is different than expected	70 %	Self-esteem lower since pastoring
80 %	Feeling unqualified/discouraged	65 %	Family lives in a "glass house"
80 %	Negatively affected their family	57 %	Unable to pay bill/need dual income
78 %	Interrupted vacation/ personal time	54 %	Pastoring feels overwhelming
72 %	Working 55-75 hrs/wk in ministry	35 %	Battling depression

These are alarming statistics for such an admirable and humble occupation and assignment. It is astonishing and grieving to read the deleterious effects that ministry can have on individuals and their families. The high rate of feeling unqualified or discouraged, or of low self-esteem, or even depression may stem from the awesome task of reconciling the role as a pastor with the calling in terms of fulfilling the leadership role as explained in the scriptures:

> *"This is a faithful saying: If a man desires the office of a bishop, he desires a good work. A bishop then must be blameless, the husband of one wife, temperate, sober-minded, of good behavior, hospitable, able to teach; not given to wine, not violent, not greedy for money; but gentle, not quarrelsome, not covetous; one who rules his own house well, having his children in submission with all reverence; (for if a man does not know how to rule his own house, how will he take care of the church of God)?"* (1 Timothy 3:1-5).

Due to these startling statistics, I sensed the need to conduct further research and interviewed pastoral families to determine a solution to decrease these dreadful outcomes. The respondents included four female spouses. One of the four serves as an assistant pastor. The pastoral children respondents were two males and one female. Two of the three are adults (one male and one female). The other male is a teenager. All respondents are of the Protestant faith, but serve in different denominations.

Findings included half of the spouses who appeared to struggle with ministry-family balance more than the other half of respondents. For example, one respondent claimed, "Surprisingly we don't have that problem…Even with the business of ministry and the needs of our congregants, we carve out family time and manage to keep a healthy family." Another respondent similarly said, "Our churches are busy. Yet we still have time for family to maintain the healthiness of our family…Having a pastoral family means you have to give back to your family as much as you take and demand." However, another respondent said, "At times I do feel like there is very little time for family. If there is time, most often it's rushed or in a hurry and not much time to relax. We are working on balance." Regarding ministry's impact on family, the other respondent described it as, "Like our lives are not our own… This one has been hard for us recently…We are currently trying to adjust." Family adjustment and children are paramount to the healthiness of pastoral families.

All three children characterized their childhood as highly scrutinized with great expectations. However, only one of the three children felt that family time suffered to a damaging extent. The female 48-year-old respondent whose parents are both pastors said, "My siblings and I often struggled with the abandonment of our parents' support during school activities because of church." The other two male respondents stated that church activities kept their parents busy, but there was still family time. These mixed findings are consistent with the idea that maintaining a healthy family balance with the ministry is something that requires active attention, thoughtful investments, and conscientious efforts.

Like some of the respondents interviewed, Dr. Steve Hall stated, "Ministry is margin-less." He warned ministers to be aware that the margin-less-ness of ministry can slowly suffocate the minister and family.[4] He stated that pastoring is the only occupation where an individual's place of work is their place of worship. The friends that pastors have are the ones who work and worship with them. The pastors' families are expected to serve where they work and worship. There is no mental-diversion for pastors and their families.

A pastor's family may feel confined in the area in which he or she is expected to love dearly. This is one reason that ministry is viewed as a dangerous career. The questions interested observers continue to ask include: Is there a proper balance between ministry and family? If so, achieving such balance requires that one faithfully shepherd a church and spend quality time with family. However, then one might ask: Is one denying God when choosing to be with family, instead of attending a church service or event?

Andrew Linder similarly explained that, although it is understandable that there will be "necessary and even intense seasons or times of staying late or working overtime…if those times ever become the majority or the norm…family is sure to notice." Linder continued to claim that family has "Every right to view it as a legitimate concern. We can't afford for the gap between what we say are our priorities, and what our family actually sees as being our priorities, to be very wide."[5] The churches and organizations that pastors lead will ultimately suffer when they do not first care for their families.

Consistent with what we read in Scriptures, the respondents surveyed explained that their families must lead by example. Scriptures provide several examples of ministry leadership and family, whereby we learn that leadership begins in the home:

> *"And these words, which I command thee today shall be in your heart. You shall teach them diligently to your children, and shall talk of them when you sit in your house, when you walk by the way, when you lie down, and when you rise up"* (Deuteronomy 6:6-7).

To fulfill these expectations and to maintain the healthiness of family, one female spouse who co-pastors with her husband shared:

Our family embraces nightly devotion (Bible) and prayer. We have always done it with our children since they were toddlers. Once a year in January, our family goes on a fast together. We make a list of prayer needs, pray over them, and revisit the list as a family at the end of the year to see how God moved…To maintain the healthiness of our family, we continuously watch movies at home; engage in meaningful, purposeful conversations; take family vacations once a year; support each other in our extra-curricular activities; we listen to each other's needs and desires in conversation and make sure we meet each other's needs. We also like to visit other people and families. We spend time together helping those who are less fortunate. It helps keep our family balanced.

Oftentimes, people attempt to categorize or separate family, church, and employment. As ministers, one is expected to serve as unto the Lord at all times (Colossians 3:17-24). One pastor shared his childhood experience growing up in a pastor's home. He spoke of significant factors that stood out that ensured a good outcome for him: "First, the relationship between my mom and dad was strong. Second, there was never a question as to my importance to the church or ministry. Third, my father shielded me from the unreasonable expectations of the congregation."[6] This pastor was intentional about the importance of balancing ministry and family.

Although ministry is demanding, and at times, consuming, God's intent for pastors is to feed, to nurture, and to lead His sheep. The sheep includes the individuals in the pastor's home. In *The Pastor's Intercessor,* the author noted, "God calls the pastor first to his family, because if the home of the pastor is not settled, it can potentially affect the pastor's ministry." Emphasized was the idea that oftentimes, the enemy will use the family to undermine the pastor; hence there is a need to always pray for pastors and their families.[7]

Many pastors feel a sense of guilt when they have chosen to attend a family event, stay home, or do a personal extracurricular activity instead of attending a church meeting or service. Some believe that they have denied God the opportunity to use them.

Some believe it is unspiritual or carnal to attend another event outside of ministry. Some believe the church or ministry cannot function without pastoral presence. All of these are unhealthy assumptions.

Throughout Scripture, God has emphasized that He has remnants to fulfill His purpose and plans (2 Kings 19:30-31; Ezra 3:8; Joel 2:32; Haggai 1:14). The biblical term "selah" found among the Psalms, indicates a pause, which some pastors likened to rest. One's absence from a ministry event does not stop God's work. If an individual is physically tired, he or she will be ineffective for ministry and the people served. This is why God established the Sabbath (Exodus 31:13-15; Leviticus 25:4). God ended His six-day creation and rested on the seventh (Genesis 2:2-3).

Busyness and Boundaries

Brian Chilton described the pastors' neglect of their families for their churches as a "disturbing trend" and called into question the practice of considering "busyness and pulling long hours" as marks of successful pastors. Chilton added, "When we learn of countless pastors who burn out from exhaustion or from those who lose their families due to neglect or infidelity, one must wonder whether this model is good after all."[8] Another question comes to mind: Why are the ones closest to the pastor neglected? The pastor may take for granted that the family will not be affected by absence or lack of attention. However, the answer may stem from perspective about what the family believes is most important—the church or the family—and then establishing boundaries accordingly.

Neglect

Neglect is defined as the failure to perform, the failure to attend to, and the failure to care for.⁹ I do not believe individuals enter ministry with the intent to disregard their loved ones. I believe once they are involved and experienced the impact of transforming other's lives, it increases their adrenaline and passion to serve more. The problem with serving more is that one does not know when to take a break or when to say no. One should never sacrifice or neglect family for ministry-sake.

Take for Granted

Usually, if the pastor's family and home are settled and in harmony, he or she assumes "all is right with the world." Or, if the church is growing, a pastor may take for granted that the family is not suffering and is also growing accordingly. Individuals taking something for granted are deducing that life and circumstances are copacetic and will remain the same. Taking something for granted means to underestimate or undervalue someone or something, or to not properly recognize or appreciate someone or something.[10]

Importance

One's interpretation of importance varies based on needs, interests, and circumstances. Importance is the quality of being of great influence or significance.[11] Winning souls for Christ is an important assignment. The goal of ministry is leading and restoring people in an eternal relationship with God; to achieve this goal requires an investment of great importance. Yet, the pastor serves a role of great importance to the family.

If the pastor's family and home are dysfunctional, it can undermine the outcomes of efforts, however great, in the church. Some pastors may over-function in one area of life to the neglect of other important areas that are taken for granted. An example discussed by Keck is doing more and more in the life of the church, in part to encourage others, but also neglecting to meet personal needs.[12] Another former pastor shared that, for the first ten years of his ministry, he was a terrific pastor but a terrible husband. He explained, "I neglected my wife. I passed on the responsibility of raising my kids ... I led my church well, and it grew by 100 people per year, yet I was not present as a leader in my own home."[13] He acknowledged taking the family for granted and living with an imbalanced view of importance that eventually spewed into the church, which ultimately caused a hindrance to the body of Christ.

It is clear, from the reported statistics, interviews of pastors and their families, and the works of notable writers, that the ministry is a vocation that often leads to a lack of boundaries between the personal and professional lives of those who respond to the calling. It is all too easy for pastors to allow their identities to be shaped not by God and their families, but by the feelings of the congregation. Pastoring is a people-focused assignment and career. Ministry can become people-driven, if we do not initially establish boundaries. Such boundaries are spiritual, mental, emotional, and physical.

Spiritual Boundaries

A pastor must remember that the relationship with Christ is first and foremost. Therefore, she or he ensures that nothing interferes with personal devotion time with God. As Christians, this is usually classified as "quiet time" with the Lord. In *Imperfect Pastor*, Zack Eswine wrote, "The purpose of quiet with God is hospitable welcome to the weary."[14] The weary are individuals who keep going and doing, while never making time to rest in the Lord (Matthew 11:28).

As an example of creating spiritual boundaries, one pastor's spouse shared "a few occasions" where she had to "be firm in the resolve to stand ground when persons have insisted that they needed to talk to the pastor and it was simply not a good time for him to speak." She further explained:

> This would occur usually before service was to begin, as he was consecrating and meditating on the sermon. Because he is so down to Earth, sometimes I feel as though people forget that he is the pastor and on Sundays, just before service, he is positioning himself to pour out what God has given him. He doesn't need anyone or anything to muddy the water. I have had to literally block the door to his study area in order to keep someone from just barging into his study.

In his discussion of pastoral fences, Kevin Conklin recommended that pastors, "Create personal and physical space to think, pray, and seek the Lord." It is important that when setting boundaries, one blocks out time with God. This time represents an appointment one would never cancel, as spending time with God is far more important than any other appointment one might want to keep.[15]

Mental Boundaries

Pastors must remember that they have limited mental capacities. One female spouse stated that some church members expect them (she and the pastor) to know what they need without telling them. They expect them to be available when needed, mentally and physically. Yet, God is the only one who is omniscient (all-knowing). Therefore, once one accepts these limitations, it should not be difficult to establish boundaries. M. Beard noted, "Mental boundaries entail one's thoughts, values, opinions, and beliefs. Trying to persuade another person can turn into a shouting match or intimidation when boundaries have been crossed."[16] Jesus modeled boundaries during His public ministry through engagement and thoughtful reflections with others. There was not a sense that Jesus was hurried nor did he fail to be fully present mentally. One must learn to be like Him by practicing healthy boundaries in relationships and with our thoughts, interactions, and mental processes applied in the commitments to the ministry.

Emotional Boundaries

A pastor must understand that usually, if one's mental boundaries have been crossed, the emotional response follows. Most times, emotion is the matter of the heart. Proverbs 4:23 says, *"Keep your heart with all diligence, for out of it spring the issues of life."* Beard further stated, "Learn how to separate your feelings from other people's feelings. Your feelings should not depend on other people's thoughts, feelings, or minds. In this way, an emotional boundary is, in most cases, one that you set on yourself."[17] Emotional boundaries are parts of healthy boundaries. Unlike scheduling boundaries, as a pastor, they are not as easy to establish and maintain.

Building healthy emotional fences may be easier for some people than for others. For example, one pastor's wife shared that initially, she thought that she was living in a fishbowl. She married her husband three years after he was appointed as pastor. She did not know her place in the ministry (outside of caring and supporting her husband). She had unhealthy emotional boundaries that disallowed her investment and sense of belonging in the ministry. After she realized that she could learn while doing, she stopped sitting back in silence, and was able to become very active and involved in the church.

One pastor's child expressed how she feels that she cannot make any mistakes. The church members expect her to live a perfect spiritual life. Pastor Hart stated in "Raising a Preacher's Kid":

> As a pastor, one cannot control the expectations that church members place upon the pastoral family, but the minister himself can make sure he does not put any additional pressures on them. Furthermore, a pastor has to be willing to take the heat from people so that his kids do not have to.[18]

Accordingly, establishing emotional boundaries are not just the responsibility of the pastor. The pastor's family members are tasked with doing the same.

Physical Boundaries

A pastor must care for and appreciate the human body. The Apostle Paul reminds us that our bodies are a temple of the Holy Spirit, which was given to us by God (1 Corinthians 6:19). Physical boundaries allow the body and mind to rest and rejuvenate to continue the works of the Lord. Jesus said, *"I must work the works of Him that sent me, while it is day: the night come, when no man can work (John 9:4)."* Yet, physical boundaries entail more than the body and extend to physical space and privacy. If this boundary is crossed, there may be an eruption of character.

In establishing boundaries, one pastor's wife stated that she and her husband purchased a home twenty or more minutes from the church. Prior to that time, they had a church member stop by their previous home and brought them live fish late in the evening during a Vacation Bible School week. He wanted to be a blessing, and he butchered the fish on their back deck. She further stated that every day, they felt like they were living in a fishbowl, and the church members had their own expectations of them being available for every possible moment of blessing, phone calls, and emergencies. Establishing physical boundaries involves communicating the understandable and appropriate need for personal and family space.

With the help of counselors, accountability partners, and his wife, Pastor Wayne Cordeiro had to learn to establish personal boundaries for himself. He called them, "My Twelve Dials." This was a tool that was essential to his health and success, after experiencing an emotional breakdown in the middle of a crosswalk. The twelve dials included such items as his faith, marriage, family, administration, ministry, finances, social, and physical domains. About the twelve dials, he said, "I first delineate what they are; then I assess them. I am brutally honest in grading each of them. I then write a few sentences that give me direction in how to make improvements." Similar to assessing strengths and weaknesses, as earlier discussed, Cordeiro assigns a letter grade to each area, and then decides which ones require immediate attention, more formal maintenance, or repair.[19]

First, He Created Family

The statistics presented at the beginning of the chapter gives one reason for concern and interest in discerning the causes for such alarming scenarios that affect the family. One pastor continuously warned, "Before God established ministry, He first created family. He never intended ministry to supersede family." I believe one of the ways to keep families joined together and not separated is developing family ministry, consistent with the saying, "A family that prays together, stays together." It also holds true for families who serve in ministry together.

While one may be the clergy, the spouse may have other gifts and talents that can be useful in the church. At the same time, couples have developed their children's skills by allowing them to serve in a ministry. An entire family involved in ministry may circumvent the chances of family members feeling neglected and of no importance. For example, one pastor's wife shared:

> While my husband serves as pastor, I serve on the worship team, as the church treasurer, and occasionally, the ladies Bible study teacher. Our two youngest children also serve on the worship team, and are members of the church's youth group. Our oldest child teaches children church.

As a family, they are very active in the church. She stated on an average Sunday, they only have three hours of home time. She said, "I feel like I am the protector of Family Time." Another female spouse stated, "From the inception of the ministry, we knew there would be times when the ministry could and would pull on our quality family time." In response, they "set things in motion, such as prayer time together, eating together as much as possible, going on dates (if only to the grocery store) and vacation time." Pastoral success within the Christian tradition is inextricably linked to the support, encouragement, and revitalization of families.

At the onset of shepherding, it is encouraged that the pastor, spouse, and children discuss the effects of ministry. Pastors need to be intentional about protecting their families and their quality time together. One never wants family to feel like an afterthought to ministry. Although Jesus stated, *"If any man come to me, and hate not his father, and mother, and wife, and children, and brethren, and sisters, yea, and his own life, he cannot be my disciple"* (Luke 14:26). In this context, He is stating that an individual is not to love and place people above Him. Loving Christ first is what gives the pastor the proper balance to care for his family's well-being, then the church. I conclude with one of the spouse's recommendations to pastoral families:

Have fun in ministry. Enjoy knowing that God has called you to perform a certain work in the area that only you can do for that season. Love the people that God sends to the ministry. BUT...NEVER let a congregant come between you and your spouse or children. Church members will come and go, but your family will be with you until you go home to be with Jesus.

The Pastor's Family

Endnotes

1. *Holman Illustrated Bible Dictionary* (Nashville: Holman Bible Publishers, 2003) 1134.
2. Ray E. Hurt, "CARE: Ministry and the Family," *Ministerial Internship Program* (Cleveland: Church of God Ministerial Development School of Ministry, 2007) 6.
3. Statistics in the Ministry," *Ministry Missing Link,* 4 Oct. 2019 https://www.pastoralcareinc.com/statistics/
4. Steve Hall, "Replenish Participant's Guide," *DELMARVA-DC Church of God* (Columbia: Church of God, 2019) 18.
5. Andrew S. Linder, "7 Practical Keys to Balancing Family, Work & Ministry," Godlyparent.com, 21 Mar. 2016, 24 Sept. 2019 http://andrewscottlinder.com/balancing-family-work-and-ministry.
6. Ray E. Hart, "Growing Up in a Pastor's Home," *Ministerial Internship Program* (Cleveland: Church of God Ministerial Development/School of Ministry, 2007) 15.
7. Aaron Jones, *The Pastor's Intercessor: Devotional Prayers for Your Pastor* (Kearney: Morris Publishing, 2011) 15.
8. Brian G. Chilton, "Pastors, don't neglect your family for your ministry," *The Christian Post,* 15 Oct. 2019 https://www.christianpost.com/voice/pastors-dont-neglect-your-family-for-your-ministry.html.
9. *The New Webster's Comprehensive Dictionary of the English Language, Deluxe Edition* (New York: Lexicon Publications, Inc. 1990) 669.
10. https://idioms.thefreedictionary.com/take+for+granted 28 Oct. 2019
11. Webster, 486.
12. David Keck, *Healthy Churches, Faithful Pastors* (Lanham: Rowman & Littlefield, 2014) 152.
13. Roger Hernandez, "When Ministry Hurts Your Family," Christianity Today, Feb. 2014, 15 Oct. 2019 https://www.christianitytoday.com/pastors/2014/february-online-only/when-ministry-hurts-your-family.html.
14. Zack Eswine, *The Imperfect Pastor* (Wheaton: Crossway, 2015) 153.
15. Conklin, K., "How Does a Busy Pastor Set Healthy Boundaries?" Focus on the Family, 9 Jan. 2020.

https://www.focusonthefamily.com/church/how-does-a-busy-pastor-set-healthy-boundaries/

16 M. Beard, "Boundaries: Definition and Types of Boundaries," *Cross Roads,* 8 Dec. 2016, 29 Oct. 2019 https://crossroadindy.com/counseling-blog/couples_and_marriage/boundaries-definition-and-types-of-boundaries.

17 Beard, 8.

18 Hart, 17.

19 Wayne Cordeiro, *Leading On Empty* (Minneapolis: Bethany House, 2009) 176.

Chapter 6
PASTORAL MINISTRY HIGHS

As stated in Chapter 5, once pastors experience the impact of changing other's lives, it increases their adrenaline and passion to serve more. Adrenaline is a pair of hormones produced by the medulla of the adrenal glands that prepares the organism for emotional stress by increasing blood pressure, elevating blood sugar level, and widening air passages in the lungs.[1] In layman's term, it is the internal organ that regulates the mind. The outward result is an individual's behavior and character operating outside of the norm. At any moment, one develops an adrenaline rush. This can be a positive or negative affect on one's brain and body. Dr. Debra Sullivan noted, "The bodily changes that occur as adrenaline circulates throughout the blood is commonly called an adrenaline rush, because these changes happen rapidly."[2] In most cases, the onset is so quick, individuals may not even fully process what is happening.

Someone may be an introvert, but an exciting or unexpected event can occur and cause this individual to act as an extrovert. This unusual behavior can be positive or negative, depending on the person and the outcome. I asked our church nurse to further explain adrenaline rush. She stated that, in any given second, someone's body responds as an alert to "fight or flight." An individual may feel an urgency to do or a desire to be inactive based on the response of the body. She noted some of the outward bodily symptoms as heart-palpitations, eyes dilating, rapid breathing, and slow digestion.

In *Leading on Empty,* Pastor Cordeiro shared a story of two encounters he had with former pastors who experienced extreme adrenaline rushes and needed to resign from pastoral ministry before it killed them. He explained that both pastors mentioned that their serotonin levels had depleted. "Serotonin is a chemical-like endorphin. It's a natural, feel-good hormone. It replenishes during times of rest and then fuels you while you're working." He warned that, "If, however, you continue to drive yourself without replenishing, your store of serotonin will be depleted. As a substitute, your body will be forced to replace the serotonin with adrenaline."[3] What is interesting is that a Christian psychologist told him, "The problem is that adrenaline is designed for emergency use only." The common explanation is that it is used for fights or for flights.

Our church psychologist described adrenaline as a surge in energy. It triggers one to feel excited, threatened, and stressed out. One's hormone activates very quickly, and the individual will experience an immediate rush or high. As pastors, ministry is multifaceted. It encompasses one's mind, body, and soul. Once one gets involved in a ministry, there is often an urgency to do more for God. There is the mindset, "I must do more to reach a lost soul." This is the pastoral ministry high.

Pastoral ministry highs are those moments of exhilaration. One is operating in a highly dependent state of mind.[4] This same term is referenced to one who uses a drug or drinks alcohol to experience a high—a state of mind that removes a person from his or her current emotional or physical state to being exogenous (out of character). As ministers, we are vessels of Christ. It is He who speaks and operates through us. The Apostle Paul told the people of Athens in Acts 17:28, *"For in Him (Jesus) we live, and move, and have our being."* The desire to help others stems from Christ. The urgency to share the Word of God to a hurting world is prompted by the Holy Spirit.

This chapter will further expound on pastoral ministry highs, the benefits, and consequences. I included peer-colleagues' personal testimonies of their pastoral ministry highs. These colleagues are all Protestant pastors with over forty years of ministry experience. These five colleagues include two females and three males. One is a bi-vocational pastor, four are full-time pastors, and two of the five oversee additional ministries outside of their pastorate. Their average church membership ranges from 100 to 500 people.

There are several phases of pastoral ministry, from the initial call of God to the additional ministerial assignments to retirement, but still doing ministry. After sixteen years of pastoring, Ron Edmondson wrote, "I learned the job can be an emotional roller coaster at times. Some days are always better than others, but learning how to deal with the highs and lows is a major key in sustaining yourself for ministry long-term."[5] A bi-vocational pastor stated, "I find myself needing multiple winds to complete the other ministries outside of my church. Time and project management are some things that I would like to do differently. One can do so much and be so ineffective." One female pastor shared her first pastoral experience, twenty-four years ago, and the emotions that occurred. She was especially concerned and "wondered if people were going to show up." After she preached her first pastoral sermon, she experienced that "adrenaline rush to continue" and "felt God's stamp of approval." She said, "I had the mindset, I'm in this, now!" Although, Scriptures tell us, *"The Lord will fight for you; you need only to be still"* (Exodus 14:14).

The Beginning of Ministry High

One may say, "My ministry high began while I was in seminary school." The gain in theological knowledge and the spiritual insight God shares with an individual can develop this high. Paul Tripp stated:

> Seminary graduates, who are Bible and theology experts,

tend to think of themselves as being mature. But it must be said that maturity is not merely something you do with your mind (although that is an important element of spiritual maturity). No, maturity is about how you live your life. It is possible to be theologically astute and be very immature.[6]

The cliché saying is, "Too much knowledge can be dangerous." It is true for ministry. On occasion, I have met individuals who are students at prominent seminaries, and as they are acquiring knowledge in Hermeneutics and Homiletics, they begin to critique their pastors and other seasoned ministers. Some have left churches and established ministries on their own, because they experienced a ministry high. Tripp shared his experience as an honors graduate of a seminary:

> I won academic awards. I assumed I was mature and felt misunderstood and misjudged by anyone who failed to share my assessment. You see, sin is not first an intellectual problem. Yes, it does affect my intellect, as it does all parts of my functioning. Sin is first a moral problem. It is about my rebellion against God and my quest to have for myself the glory that is due to him.[7]

A problem with ministry high is that it is possible to lose sight of whom one is serving. Ministers may become so engulfed (adrenaline rush) in appearing as biblical and theological experts, they may think that ministry is about them and not God.

One may be surprised, but servant-leaders have spunk; yet, this spunk needs channeling in righteous directions to continue to serve God and not oneself. Dr. Richard Krejoir stated, "Spunk is the willingness to take a risk and go beyond ourselves, our experience and knowledge and into what is the best for the body of Christ!"⁸ Jesus choosing to lay down His divine nature and take on a human nature was a risk (Philippians 2:6). Choosing to be a propitiation for us on the cross, just so that we may have eternal life, was a major risk (1 John 2:2). Servant-leaders consider the sacrificial cost, but are willing to take the risk to help others and must not lose sight of their initial motivations that ultimately led to the beginning of a ministry high. Servant-leaders establish their confidence in Christ. They know that their identity and abilities are not based on them, but on the Spirit of God who resides in them.

Scriptures are very clear that nothing is revealed or made known unless God shares it. *"The secret things belong unto the Lord our God: but those things which are revealed belong unto us and to our children forever, that we may do all the words of this law"* (Deuteronomy 29:29). All biblical and theological knowledge is gained through God. *"Surely the Lord God will do nothing, but He revealeth His secrets unto His servants the prophets"* (Amos 3:7). Biblical and theological knowledge is revealed to the servants of God. *"But God hath revealed them unto us by His Spirit: for the Spirit searcheth all things, yea, the deep things of God"* (1 Corinthians 2:10).

Therefore, individuals have to establish a proper balance in the ministry high. It is amazing when one sees God's word manifested in other's lives and communities being transformed. There is an impetus to studying Scriptures more and seeking numerous opportunities to preach and teach. A male full-time pastor shared his first ministry experience: "The way I saw God moving in the services and touching people's lives (even young people), their hunger for God and His presence was very exciting for me." This excitement (adrenaline rush) leads to the perceived need to do even more.

Servant-leaders are go-getters. They are always seeking opportunities to serve more. They are not content unless they are blessing or developing others. Servant-leaders understand Luke 12:48, *"For everyone to whom much is given, from Him much will be required; and to whom much has been committed, of Him they will ask the more."* They are never complacent and afraid to move to the next area of ministry that God ordains. As God advances them, servant-leaders prepare others to succeed them. That is where their satisfaction is derived but can also be where the ministry high begins.

Another individual may believe that this ministry high began when serving the community via food and clothes distribution or a mission trip to a foreign country. Meeting the physical needs of others causes one to identify with Christ. Jesus as stated in a parable in Matthew 25:40, *"Verily I say unto you, Inasmuch as ye have done it unto one of the least of these my brethren, ye have done it unto me."* Individuals serving in an outreach ministry are operating as God's outstretched hand to a hurting or disadvantaged community. Again, once one blesses another, she or he wants to continuously be a blessing. Unfortunately, there are times when financial and physical resources hinder one from doing so. Therefore, the ministry and its resources are overextended (adrenaline rush).

Middle of the Ministry High

Ministering God's word to individuals and groups can be exuberating. Providing and assisting those who are less fortunate are rewarding. In *Uncharted Waters,* the author tells of the life and ministry of Bishop Raymond Crowley. In this biography, Bishop Crowley preached his first revival at the age of fifteen. At sixteen, he pastored his church and was appointed state superintendent of Sunday School and YPE. At seventeen, he married and moved to pastor his second congregation; and at eighteen, he and his new bride moved and pastored their third congregation.[9] Ministry is progressive. A minister may begin his ministry call in one setting, and without planning, finds himself serving in other capacities.

There are additional instances where pastoral ministry highs occur in different capacities. Pastor Cordeiro served in ministry for over thirty years. His drive (adrenaline rush) for excellence propelled him. He stated that he wasn't compulsive. He simply had a deep desire to do his best. He pioneered a church and became the senior pastor. He started several other churches, which led to him becoming the director of church planting. He planted over a hundred churches. In addition, he desired to train emerging leaders and became the president of a Bible college. He authored eight books and developed a magazine.[10] Pastor Steve Austin recounted his equally busy life, sustained physically through the rush of adrenaline:

> At one point, I was a youth pastor, professional sign language interpreter, wedding photographer, radio host, husband, and father. As an interpreter, I worked full time in a public school, including all of my student's after-school activities. My radio show consumed Tuesday and Friday nights. Wednesday nights and all-day Sunday were eaten up by church functions, and Saturdays were spent photographing weddings, with youth group activities, or both. Long days and late nights were the norm.[11]

Pastor Sam Rima's first assignment as a senior pastor was with a newly forming congregation in a rapidly developing community. The small group of excited believers had no building of their own, no office facility for a pastor, and not even the financial resources to pay a salary. It was a tailor-made situation for a person to please and see tangible signs of success. Unfortunately, that standard of success was reduced to numeric growth and economic expansions.

Rima said, "As long as I could keep the ministry expanding in ways that my board and denominational superiors could see, I felt a measure of approval."[12] Feelings of approval from hard work were similar to the rush felt by surges of adrenaline.

Deep in Ministry Highs

There are blessings to serving in ministry and from coaching and mentoring others, traveling around the world, and providing resources to the disadvantaged. It is in these moments that a minister seizes every opportunity afforded. Pastor Zack stated, "Like many of my colleagues, I craved making an epic difference for God in my vocation as fast as possible."[13] His emphasis was on epic. He questioned himself, "Why not ordinary?" Oddly, ordinary doesn't sound as inviting or influential as epic. Webster's definition of ordinary is not exceptional or unusual, undistinguished.[14] Alternatively, epic is a long narrative poem conceived on a grand scale, telling a story of great or heroic deeds.[15]

Unfortunately, many ministers (including pastors) begin with an ordinary perspective of ministry, but after experiencing the accolades and some fame, they find themselves deep in ministry highs and are unable to separate from it. Tripp noted:

> Pastoral ministry was exciting in many ways. The church was growing numerically and people seemed to be growing spiritually. More and more people seemed to be committing to this vibrant spiritual community, and we saw battles of the heart taking place in people's lives. We founded a Christian school, which was growing and expanding its reputation and influence. We were beginning to identify and disciple leaders. It wasn't all rosy, and there were moments that were painful and burdensome, but I started

out my days with a deep sense of privilege that God had called me to do what he had called me to do.[16]

Most ministers have the humility and amazement like the Apostle Paul who said, *"I thank Christ Jesus our Lord, who hath enabled me, for that He counted me faithful, putting me into the ministry"* (1 Timothy 1:12). The ministry high comes from the astonishment that God would entrust His spiritual knowledge and abilities to transform other's lives. Sadly, there are times when ministers and pastors become so enamored by the busyness of ministry that they may lose control of one's self physically, mentally, and spiritually. One colleague shared his recent experience of needing a "second wind" in pastoral ministry:

> As a senior pastor, in 2017, I was putting too much stress and pressure on myself to grow the church. At the same time, there were some staff challenges that were draining the life out of me. Coming out of that experience has been eye-opening. Even though God didn't cause it, He did meet me there. I have been very intentional over the past two years to make the needed adjustments to myself, my schedule, the church, and the leadership/staff. So I do not hit that kind of wall again.

Increases in memberships and church attendances are one of the highs of pastoral ministry. The idea that God has entrusted numerous individuals in one's care can be astounding. The pastor's heart is aligned with the numerous methods to keep the sheep in the fold. What happens as a result of receiving much is doing more, and doing more than one is physically able. Rima said:

> Unfortunately, many Christian leaders are driven manically

to have success. In the church, having success is measured by how many people you have attending your service, the size of the facility you have, the number of staff members you have, how many user-friendly programs you have, and the size of the budget you have. As a result, leaders who need to have success to validate themselves are driven to acquire these things and are willing to pay virtually any price to do so.[17]

Drowning in Ministry Highs

There are other times that pastors enjoy the material and notoriety benefits of ministry and lose sight of Christ, which later result in self-gratification and self-glorification. Chuck Lawless noted in *The Christian Post* that, "The more successful pastors are, the easier it is to assume, that will never happen to me."[18] He concluded that the number one reason for pastors' failings is success.

As previously stated, most individuals called to ministry respond with a heart of integrity. A heart to win people to Christ. They enter ministry with a heart and mind to share the gospel and love of God. For example, the consensus response from my five colleagues was that their first ministry experience was fearful, yet exciting. They wanted to please God, speak well before the audience, and experience God's approval. The related question therefore is: When does the desire to please God shift to pleasing one's self?

Eswine explained that one may spend more time doing ministry and less time with God. He shared the suicide of his pastor/mentor, who killed himself amidst everything that most would call success. Eswine warned, "But sometimes ministry things that we desire in our culture are not the same as the mattering things Jesus gives us." Similar to what we tell our businesspeople "that it is empty to gain the whole world but lose their souls," is it possible in vocational ministry to do the same?[19]

God's intent for pastors is to feed, lead, and nurture His sheep. All additional assignments that one, as a pastor, assumes are additions to building God's kingdom; but they are not priorities. Grievously, some pastors become charmed by the gained personal influence that, they find themselves drowning in ministry highs and floating away from the life-preserver, Jesus Christ. Some examples of ministry highs are the motivation to building larger facilities, expanding ministries beyond the local church, broadcasting or televising services, and hosting mega-conferences, among others. Eswine explained, "Our desire for greatness in ministry isn't the problem. Our problem rises from how the haste of doing large things, famously and as fast as we can, is reshaping our definition of what a great thing is." The solution is to "Desire greatness, dear pastor! But bend your definition of greatness to the one Jesus gives us."[20] Pastors must preach for God's glory and not one's own.

Initially, a pastor's motive for greatness is honorable, and the intentions are good. It is when the drive becomes misdirected and distracted from the gospel message that the pastor begins to drown and sink into a ministry low. In the next chapter, I will present pastors' ministry lows and the effects it has on them and their ministries.

Endnotes

1. *The New Webster's Comprehensive Dictionary of the English Language, Deluxe Edition* (New York: Lexicon Publications, Inc. 1990) 6.
2. Debra Sullivan, PhD, MSN, RN, CNE, COI, "Adrenaline Rush: Everything You Should Know," *healthline* 1 Nov. 2018, 2 Nov. 2019 https://www.healthline.com/health/adrenaline-rush#causes.
3. Wayne Cordeiro, *Leading On Empty* (Minneapolis: Bethany House, 2009) 25.
4. Webster, 457.
5. Ron Edmondson, "4 Suggestions for Balancing the Highs and Lows of Ministry," *ChurchLeaders* 10 Aug. 2018, 4 Nov. 2019 https://churchleaders.com/pastors/pastor-articles/330674-4-suggestions-balancing-the-highs-and-lows-of-ministry-Ron-Edmondson.html.
6. Paul David Tripp, *Dangerous Calling* (Wheaton: Crossway, 2012) 25.
7. Ibid, 26.
8. Richard J. Krejoir, Ph.D., "Effective Leadership Have Spunk," Schaeffer Institute of Church Leadership, 12 Jan. 2020 http://www.churchleadership.org/apps/articles/default.asp?articleid=41894&columnid=4540.
9. Philip and Mary Morris, *Uncharted Waters: The Life & Ministry of Raymond E. Crowley* (Cleveland: Pathway Press, 2014) 40.
10. Cordeiro, 21-22.
11. Steven Austin, *From Pastor to a Psych Ward* (Middletown: Steve Austin, 2016) 33.
12. Gary L. McIntosh and Samuel D. Rima, *Overcoming the Dark Side of Leadership* (Grand Rapids: Baker Books, 2007) 31.
13. Zack Eswine, *The Imperfect Pastor* (Wheaton: Crossway, 2015) 21.
14. Webster, 706.
15. Webster, 316.
16. Tripp, 27.
17. McIntosh and Rima, 20.
18. Chuck Lawless, "8 reasons long-term pastors still fail," *The Christian Post*, 11 Nov. 2019 https://www.christianpost.com/voice/8-reasons-long-term-pastors-still-fail.html.
19. Eswine, 42.
20. Ibid, 29.

Chapter 7
PASTORAL MINISTRY LOWS

When the occupation an individual once loved so much becomes a daily dread, this is a low in one's life. Lows are those bad and difficult moments, the states of depression, and a decline in spirit.[1] One may ask, "How can God's work be a low to a pastor?" It is in the same manner that ministers experience a high in impacting other's lives that they experience ministry lows. Some causes of a pastor's ministry lows are decline in church memberships and attendances, loss of leadership support, inflated church budgets, decline in tithes and offerings, and individuals' constant expectations and demands.

Reexamining the statistics from *Ministry Missing Link,* we can appreciate that 84% of pastors felt they are on call 24/7 and 90% of pastors reported that ministry is completely different than what they thought it would be before entering the ministry. Three-quarters of pastors surveyed reported significant stress-related crisis at least once in their ministry. Approximately half felt overworked and unable to meet their church's unrealistic expectations and identified the biggest challenge as recruiting volunteers and encouraging their members to change (living closer to God's Word).

There is an unstated assumption that working for the church is easy and stress-less, but the same rule that applies in the marketplace holds true in the church: "Wherever there are people, there are problems." No one can dictate or control others' behaviors. Just as the economy affects society and the workforce, the church is also affected. However, Jack Morris stated:

> Pastoring is the most appreciated and unappreciated of occupations at once. We can soar to great heights or

fall to new depths within moments of an encouraging compliment or a negative remark. I speak from personal experience, having been a pastor for more than fifty years.[2]

Ministry is serving people. Pastoral ministry is leading, guiding, and nurturing people. All aspects of ministry require an individual's whole being (mind, soul, and body). No one enters ministry without expecting to give their all to God and the people. The problem lies when the gospel message is rejected, when demands are greater than supplies, when one loses focus and forgets the original vision, and when one declines in a relationship with Christ.

Rejection

In the 21st century, churches are competing with society's new norms. In earlier decades and centuries, attending church was a priority. Sundays were viewed as a sacred day. Businesses were closed and families gathered together for worship services. Yet, the concepts of religiosity and spirituality continue to change, along with the placement of them as priorities in the lives of contemporary youth and adults. As we draw closer to Christ's return, daily, Scripture is revealed. The Apostle Paul admonished pastors:

> "*Preach the word; be instant in season, out of season; reprove, rebuke, exhort with all longsuffering and doctrine. For the time will come when they will not endure sound doctrine; but after their own lusts shall they heap to themselves teachers, having itching ears; and they shall turn away their ears from the truth, and shall be turned unto fables*" (2 Timothy 4:2-4).

Preston Sprinkles explained that modern churches have changed in how it views others, how monies are spent, how power is viewed, and how the Bible is read.[3] In the early Church, there was usually one service time. A church having more than one service on a Sunday was usually for special occasions, such as Easter and Christmas. Ed Stetzer noted that, "Some churches have moved to multiple services for strategic reasons—like engaging their community."[4] Churches more recently established multiple services for numerous reasons from people's preferences to ministry missions. Such advances add stress to a pastor.

Engaging the community is becoming the rule and not the exception. On any given Sunday, schools are hosting sporting events during worship service times. Parents are accommodating children's extra-curricular activities and attending churches that have multiple service times or not attending at all. Responding to the competition, pastors and leaders are seeking methods and alternatives to encourage weekly attendances and commitments to Christ.

One of my pastoral colleagues stated that a ministry low is the fact that sometimes members do not have the same passion for ministry. Wanting to see the gospel and the witnessing of the church in full force, it is not displayed, which emotionally bothers her. Carey Nieuwhof wrote, "Churches just have people in them. And that makes it…well, complex."[5] It is complex because true ministry is out of one's control. Everything that one does is submitted to God's leadership. Ministers understand that service is unto the Lord, and not for selfish gain or glory. Therefore, an intimate relationship with Christ and constant communication are crucial for effective ministry. Some of the lows occur, when one's humble service is rejected, abused, unappreciated, misunderstood, or misinterpreted.

Demands

When there is a need in the community, one of the first places a person seeks assistance is the church. Churches are visually seen in the neighborhoods. Most churches are known as a valuable resource to those who are less fortunate or in a disadvantage state. Most individuals believe that they do not have to go through the red-tape to receive immediate assistance. About meeting these demands, Ruben Exantus wrote, "Shepherding a spiritual flock is not so simple; it comes with a price tag. True leadership, even when it is practiced by the most mature and emotionally stable person, always exacts a toll on him or her."[6] Pastors view people as God's children and this tradition of care originates from the Scriptures:

> *"For I was an hungry and you gave me food; I was thirsty and you gave me drink; I was a stranger and you took me in; I was naked and you clothed me; I was sick and you visited me; I was in prison and you came to me"* (Matthew 25:35-36).

The conclusion of this parable is these benevolent acts towards others are actions being done to Jesus. Therefore, a pastor's heart and passion is to care for people. Unfortunately, the pastor is only one person, in need of assistance from others to fulfill this mission. In most communities, the needs are greater than the church's ability to supply. Therefore, the pastor may overextend oneself or the church's resources. Paul Tripp said that this is the point when, "Ministry stops being about worship and becomes an ever-repeating series of pastoral responsibilities."[7] This becomes an additional stress and ministry low.

Another area of demands stems from the membership (individuals who have chosen to be a part or affiliated with a church), who have pastoral and church expectations. Some requests and expectations are warranted; but other times, they can be unreasonable and indoctrinate. Keck wrote, "One challenge facing pastors and congregations is the simple fact that not everyone in a congregation understands what it is like to be a pastor. (Similarly, pastors often make the mistake of thinking everyone should think like they do!)"[8] Therefore, communication from both parties is crucial.

At my church, one of the new member classes is "Understanding Your Pastor." The class is designed to teach each new member the roles of the pastor according to Scriptures. It is explained in five parts: (a) Pastor as a Leader, (b) Pastor as a Bishop, (c) Pastor as a Prophet, (d) Pastor as an Evangelist, and (e) Pastor as a Shepherd. Each section allows the members to biblically see God's intent for the pastor, and their role as members is to pray and intercede for their pastor. The desired goal is that the members would partner with the pastor to fulfill the church's divine plan for the community, and not assume that it is only the pastor's job to serve. Regrettably, the goal is not always successfully met, contributing to a pastoral low.

One colleague stated that a pastoral low for him is when people drain the life out of him and he does not see any fruit (spiritual development). He added, "There is no return of spiritual life to the church. It's disappointing!" A common response from two additional colleagues was the pain of people leaving the church, not because they have been sent to establish a ministry, but because they left for no apparent reason. Both pastors stated that it is usually the individuals with whom they have spent extreme amounts of time in discipleship that most disappoint when they leave. They both noted that these departures are expected in the pastoral role; but, it does not stop the emotional pain because it touches the heart.

Lose Focus

Since ministry is multifaceted, it is easy for one to desire more. Eswine claimed, "As you enter ministry, you will be tempted to orient your desires toward doing large things in famous ways as fast and as efficiently as you can." However, Eswine added, "But take note, a crossroads waits for you. Jesus is that crossroads. Because almost anything in life that truly matters will require you to do small, mostly overlooked things, over a long period of time with him."[9] The problem with small is that it sometimes can be conventional and mundane. If the pastorate appears to be cumbersome and ineffective within the church and community, the pastor begins to seek additional ministry opportunities.

At that time, the pastor's primary focus may shift from caring and leading the sheep to ministry expansion. Ministry expansion can include such activities as outside speaking engagements, facilitating trainings and conferences, and world mission projects, among others. All of these ministry assignments are commendable and fruitful; however, when they become a pastor's principal interest, instead of shepherding the appointed sheep, a pastoral ministry low lurks. One may no longer be satisfied in the call. Pastor Cordeiro stated:

> I hadn't realized that as a pastor, I was involved in a vocation that had a dismal track record. It might be the pressures involved, or it could be the high expectations. But in either case, I found that a large number of those in pastoral ministry did not finish well.[10]

Inconsistent Relationship

When one loses sight of the vision, there can be a wandering of heart and relationships. The busyness of ministry causes one to operate on intellect and strength, and no longer rely on the all-sufficient One, Christ. Ministry is no longer about God and His plan, but about self and selfish agendas. Hence, the relationship between the pastor and God is challenged. Ministry is no longer soul-focused, but now self-driven. In *"3 Occupational Hazards for Pastors,"* Dr. Doriani stated that adulation invites narcissism. He explained that one pastor confessed, "Praise is the success of ministry. It's tempting to believe the accolades."[11] A resultant danger can be the temptation to become self-aggrandizing rather than God-glorifying.

Yes, everyone appreciates acknowledgements and words of appreciation, but when the appreciation becomes self-gratification, one has forgotten the One served. The mission of the pastoral call has shifted from shepherding to hireling. Thus is the reason God addressed the Old Testament shepherds: *"Woe be unto the pastors that destroy and scatter the sheep of my pasture! Saith the Lord"* (Jeremiah 23:1). And, *"Thus saith the Lord God; Woe unto the foolish prophets, that follow their own spirit, and have seen nothing!" (Ezekiel 13:3).* Again, God's original intent for pastors is to feed, lead, and care for His sheep. *"Son of man, prophesy against the shepherds of Israel, prophesy, and say unto them, Thus saith the Lord God unto the shepherds; Woe be to the shepherds of Israel that do feed themselves! Should not the shepherds feed the flocks?"* (Ezekiel 34:2). Any additional ministry assignments are assets to the kingdom of God, but are not the pastor's primary call.

Additional ministry assignments break the monotony and frustration of the pastorate, but may also be so consuming that one loses both self and a relationship with God. Time spent in prayer and devotion begins to become less or obsolete. *Ministry Missing Link* revealed that 95% of the pastors surveyed report not praying daily or regularly with their spouse and 50% of pastors stated they spend one hour in prayer each day.[12] One's decreased time with God results in the lack of humility and confessions of sins. Sin is action by which humans rebel against God, miss His purpose for their life, and surrender to the power of evil rather than God.[13]

This broken communion causes a broken relationship, not only with God, but also with everyone who is connected to the pastor. Thus, what emerges is another pastoral ministry low.

Corrupt and Immoral Behavior

In pastoral ministry lows, the more disconnected the pastor becomes, the more subjection to sin arises. Nieuwhof said, "As a leader, I have to make sure I continue to confess my sins before God daily. Confession is designed to stop what sin starts."[14] Thoughts may arise about how many engagements one can obtain, how much a church may be willing to pay for speaking, or how many will attend service or conference. Finding oneself absorbed in "me, my, and I," ministry is no longer about God and His plans. In the *Gospel Coalition,* Jim Davis reminds us that, "For the at-risk-pastor, ministry exists to serve Him, not the other way around."[15] Although the pastor is serving in ministry, the intent is no longer driven by soul-winning, but selfish wins that can manifest as sins.

The distance away from God results in corrupt and immoral behavior as a believer. Nieuwhof shared a conversation he had with a pastor who had to resign because of an affair: "I asked him why he had an affair, and he told me in part it was because he couldn't find an easy way to get out. The affair forced him out." One may ask why the pastor did not just choose to stop doing ministry and find another career. The problem lies in the inconsistent relationship with God. Ministry busyness, plus the drive to become more, minus quality time with God, equals moral and physical destruction. Quality time with God allows one's spiritual sensitivity (discernment) to increase. God always forewarns before a downfall occurs. Proverbs 16:18 says, *"Pride goes before destruction, and a haughty spirit before a fall."* God is gracious and merciful to all mankind, but after several warnings and no adherence, consequences occur.

Scriptures allow us to hear the heartbeat of God. Reading and meditating on Scriptures is the act of looking in a spiritual mirror. McIntosh and Rima claimed that a troubling reality about today's spiritual leaders is the "increasing number of them who do not consistently devote time to personal spiritual disciplines. Too many leaders today do not regularly expose themselves to the scrutinizing probe of the Holy Spirit by looking into Scripture."[16] The Word of God is our standard for living. So often, we as ministers and pastors can become so accustom to reading the Bible for the purpose of preaching, and do not allow it to minister to us. Tripp says, "This is a dangerous place to be; it puts your heart at risk, but this is the place where many, many pastors work and live."[17] As a result, it distances our relationship with the Author of the Book, causing a pastoral ministry low.

In closing, there are numerous pastoral ministry lows. Consequently, the purpose of this chapter was to cause an awareness of the leadership threats that a pastor faces, to return the busy pastor to the first love (quality time with God), and to inspire the parishioners to pray daily for their pastors. In the next chapter are warning signs related to pastoral destruction and devastations, looking at the symptoms, the consequences, and the outcomes, if unheeded, undiagnosed, and unresolved.

Endnotes

1. *The New Webster's Comprehensive Dictionary of the English Language, Deluxe Edition* (New York: Lexicon Publications, Inc. 1990) 588.
2. H. Jack Morris, "The superhuman pastor," *Ministry Magazine*, Jan. 2019, 11 Nov. 2019 https://www.ministrymagazine.org/archive/2019/01/The-superhuman-pastor.
3. Preston Sprinkles, "4 Ways the Modern Church Looks Nothing Like the Early Church," *Relevant Magazine*, 12 Nov. 2019, 15 Nov. 2019 https://relevantmagazine.com/god/4-ways-modern-church-looks-nothing-early-church/.
4. Ed Stetzer, "Should Churches Have Multiple Worship Service Styles? Consumerism or Contextualization?," *Christianity Today*, 27 Sept. 2011, 15 Nov. 2019 https://www.christianitytoday.com/edstetzer/2011/september/should-churches-have-multiple-worship-service-styles.html.
5. Carey Nieuwhof, "Some Thoughts About the Recent Exit of Two Megachurch Pastors," Sept. 2016, 12 Nov. 2019 https://Carey Nieuwhof.com/some-thoughts-about-the-recent-exit-of-two-megachurch-pastors/.
6. W. Ruben Exantus, Ph.D., *Pastoral Burnout and Leadership Styles* (Bloomington:AuthorHouse, 2012) xvi.
7. Paul David Tripp, *Dangerous Calling* (Wheaton: Crossway, 2012) 35.
8. David Keck, Healthy Churches, *Faithful Pastors* (London: Rowman & Littlefield, 2014) 41.
9. Zack Eswine, *The Imperfect Pastor* (Wheaton: Crossway, 2015) 26.
10. Wayne Cordeiro, *Leading On Empty* (Minneapolis: Bethany House, 2009) 32.
11. Dan Doriani, "3 Occupational Hazards for Pastors," *The Gospel Coalition,* 23 Jul. 2015, 19 Nov. 2019 https:///www.thegospelcoalition.org/article/3-occupational-hazards-for-pastors/.
12. Statistics in the Ministry," 2.
13. *Holman Illustrated Bible Dictionary* (Nashville: Holman Bible Publishers, 2003) 1505.
14. Carey Nieuwhof, "5 Reasons Pastors Fail Morally (And What to Watch For in Your Own Life)," Careynieuwhof.com, Aug. 2014,

19 Nov. 19 https://careynieuwhof.com/5-reasons-pastors-fail-morally-and-what-to-watch-for-in-your-own-life/.

15 Jim Davis, "5 Signs You're an At-Risk Pastor," *The Gospel Coalition*, 8 Oct. 2019, 19 Nov. 2019 https://www.thegospelcoalition.org/article/5-signs-you're-at-risk-pastor?.

16 Gary L. McIntosh and Samuel D. Rima, *Overcoming the Dark Side of Leadership* (Grand Rapids: Baker Books, 2007) 199-200.

17 Tripp, 195.

Chapter 8
WARNING SIGNS

An individual's responsibility for the spiritual lives of others, while managing a church's finance and administration, can be causes of intense stress. O.S. Hawkins stated, "There is high anxiety in the high calling of ministry. The pressures of the pastorate are especially intense breeding grounds for stress."[1] A pastor never wants to be the one to cause individuals to no longer have a relationship with Jesus Christ. The passion is to be of spiritual assistance, not of spiritual hindrance, to anyone's Christian walk. Also, one never wants to be a bad steward of God's resources. When a pastor sees sheep going astray, or God's church becoming dysfunctional, it becomes personal.

The problem with caring so much is that the pastor, sometimes, does not know when to step back, release, and allow God to do the work in the lives of the people and the ministry. There are times when the pastor has given all to the church and the parishioners, and may experience a physical or character attack. The pastor becomes emotionally and spiritually wounded. One tries to press pass the pain and continue to walk in Christlikeness, but trust in people may wane. Lastly, a pastor's thrive for ministry success may cause one to take on more than God intends. The more influence and impact a pastor experiences, the more she or he may do, which can overextend both oneself and the church.

This chapter will include the symptoms of burnout, emotional trauma, over-zealousness, and egotism. I researched stress warning signs, the negative and positive outcomes, suggested plans of action for pastors, and recommendations to parishioners to encourage pastoral care. I interviewed six pastoral colleagues who are Protestant pastors (four males and two females). Their pastorate experience ranged from four years to thirty-one years. These pastors serve in other ministry capacities outside of their churches. They provided a variety of perspectives on the stress of ministry, discerning the warning signs, and the favorable and unfavorable outcomes.

Leading the Sheep Astray

There are numerous statistics about pastors leaving ministry in record-breaking numbers. However, Mark Dance with *LifeWay* disagreed. He wrote, "It is a prevailing myth that 1,500 to 1,700 pastors leave the ministry every month. The promising truth is 250 pastors leave the ministry every month."[2] Whether the number is in the thousands or in the hundreds, it is disheartening, because while pastors leave the ministry, 23.1% of Americans claim no religion[3] and 16% of the world's population is not affiliated with a religion.[4] The heart of Christian ministry is reaching souls for Christ. Scriptures state that God desires that no soul would perish, but all would come into repentance (2 Peter 3:9). Yet, Scriptures also warn, *"'Woe to the shepherds who destroy and scatter the sheep of My pasture!' declares the LORD"* (Jeremiah 23:1).

Although ministry functions in various forms, it is the pastor who teaches and encourages believers to love and live for Christ and to reach others who have never heard or experienced Him. However, Jeremiah 50:6 warned, *"My people have been lost sheep. Their shepherds have led them astray, turning them away on the mountains. From mountain to hill they have gone. They have forgotten their fold."* It is true that one person should not have so great of an influence on others. However, the fact is that there are many believers who are not spiritually-mature to grow in their own relationship with Christ. Thus, the purpose of a pastor continues in response to the call. Such dependency can lead to the stress symptoms that a pastor experiences. If a pastor loses the passion

The Warning Signs

for ministry, it is possible that it will affect the parishioners. Sheep follow their shepherd.

Burnout

One may be so engulfed in ministry call that it becomes easy to ignore the extreme emotional and interpersonal stressors that represent the warning signs for positive change. Christina Maslach and her colleagues stated, "Occupational burnout is a prolonged response to chronic emotional and interpersonal stressors on the job, and is defined by the three dimensions of exhaustion, cynicism, and inefficacy."[5] Sadly, pastors may come to believe they are failing God when they lose the drive to serve His people.

The foundation of pastoral leadership is deeply rooted in the pastor's calling. Exantus described it as a threefold calling: (a) a pastor's call to salvation; (b) a pastor's call to service; and (c) a pastor's call to full-time ministry.[6] In each of these calls, the pastor has to be intentional about knowing God's people, to pattern life to serve like Jesus, and to become available when needed. Yet, even in serving like Jesus, the pastor has to establish a proper balance.

In all the work and miracles Jesus performed, He always established physical and spiritual balance. Revisiting the idea of spiritual, physical, and emotional boundaries, there are many Biblical examples. *"Now in the morning, having risen a long while before daylight, He went out and departed to a solitary place; and there He prayed"* (Mark 1:35). Jesus is attending to the spiritual boundary. *"And He said to them, 'Come aside by yourselves to a deserted place and rest a while.' For there were many coming and going, and they did not even have time to eat. So they departed to a deserted place in the boat by themselves"* (Mark 6:31-32). They were attending to physical boundaries. *"Come to Me, all you who labor and are heavy laden, and I will give you rest. Take My yoke upon you and learn from*

Me, for I am gentle and lowly in heart, and you will find rest for your souls. For My yoke is easy and My burden is light" (Matthew 11:28-30). Emotional balance stems from care and attention to rest the heart, soul, and mind.

After extreme times of ministry, Jesus always seized opportunities for solitude, replenishment, and restoration. In God's pastoral call to man, He never required one to function beyond his or her physical and mental capabilities. That is why God established the Sabbath. Sabbath is a day of rest. Considered holy to God by His rest on the seventh day after creation, the Sabbath is viewed as a sign of the covenant relation between God and His people and of the eternal rest He has promised them.[7]

Yet, when a pastor pushes beyond one's natural capabilities, the occupational burnout emerges. Some of the burnout warning signs are becoming extremely exhausted, easily irritated and offended, and lacking in ministry zeal or sensitivity. One of the pastoral colleagues who served as a senior pastor for fourteen years stated, "The warning signs of burnout and high anxiety were extreme fatigue, at times, and irritability. I lacked sabbatical and rest, and I felt like I was failing." Pastors should learn and recognize the warning signs of burnout before it manifests itself. One of the biggest indicators is when one's emotional response to situations are "out of proportion to how a balanced person would respond."[8]

Another colleague, who had been pastoring for thirty-one years stated that a clinical pastoral counselor called the negative outcomes he was experiencing Post Traumatic Stress Pastoring (PTSP). "Phone calls from certain people and various kinds of innocent comments instantly created feelings of anxiety for me." Until he recognized it for what it was, he was unable to push through to a more peaceful and healthy thought process. The keyword to addressing burnout is *recognize*. One must recognize and understand that humans are finite beings who were created to rest. "Professional ministry has a terrible tendency to valorize overworking as virtue. Overwork does not serve our people any more than it serves us."[9] If Jesus felt the need to rest, the pastor needs to also.

Emotional Trauma

The weight of the pastorate involves emotional rollercoasters. One day, the pastor feels able to save the world. Within minutes, there is an all-time low as the same pastor wants to hide away from church and family. Even if well-versed in Scripture with the power of God flowing through them, pastors still face moments of despair. Both of the female pastoral colleagues stated that they were traumatized by people stating that they were leaving the church. One pastor explained, "Even though, they said I wasn't the reason, I began to feel like I had done something wrong." Some parishioners have great admiration and respect for pastors, while others have their opinions and no regard for them or their calling. This can lead to emotional trauma.

Emotional and psychological trauma is the result of extraordinarily stressful events that shatter a sense of security, leading to feelings of helplessness in a dangerous world. Traumatic experiences often involve a threat to life or safety, but any situation that leaves you feeling overwhelmed and isolated can result in trauma, even if it doesn't involve physical harm.[10] A pastor's traumatic experience may be character assassination from parishioners. The same tenured pastor, who was previously quoted, shared an experience where members of the congregation held secret meetings to discuss their views of how the church was doing. In every case, what followed was an effort to recruit others to complain. These failed attempts to disrupt the church were led by disgruntled people leaving the church and attempts to persuade others to leave with them. Although each of their attempts to affect the general congregation failed, the pastor described being stricken with anxiety.

Many people cannot comprehend that the weight of ministry is beyond an average 9-to-5 job. A pastor's assignment does not end on Sundays after preaching. It has been said by several pastors, "After preaching one or more services on Sunday, at the end of the day, I experience depression." One would hear the congregation gasp from shock. No one truly knows the emotional trauma a pastor experiences except another pastor. This emotional strain does not only occur with new pastors, but also with those who have been shepherding for over thirty or more years. Keck noted:

> Pastors get so caught up in their work that their emotional well-being can depend almost entirely on their congregations. When the people say 'good job!' they feel good, but when the people do not respond with praise and gratitude, they wonder, 'Am I a bad pastor or even a bad person? Why don't they like me more?'[11]

The pastoral call warrants all forms of responses from people. One minute, they are loving the pastor as their preacher, but in seconds that may change. Many people may love the emotional high and charismatic experience of the preached word, but some do not want to be held accountable to it. This is when the emotional trauma occurs.

The pastor's role as shepherd is to help the parishioners to live out the preached word. This role requires additional days and time spent with the people. There are some church attenders who will hear the sermon and apply it to their daily living. There are others who need hand-holding and spiritual guidance to trust God and take Him at His word. Then, there are those who have no intention of application and expect the pastor to provide the solutions to their problems. However, Tripp said, "I love helping pastors to see that their security is not to be found in how much the people of their church will come to love them, but in the reality of how much Jesus already has loved them."[12] Despite such revelation, sadly pastors may become bipolar, tripartite, or dissociative in response to feelings of insecurity.

Two of the colleagues stated that their church's financial challenges caused them to have sleepless nights. It was not until they released their concerns to God and watched Him send forth provisions that they were able to pastor in peace. The weight of being ultimately responsible for the financial and spiritual well-being of the church brings anxiety. When the church is doing well, society credits the pastor; and, when the church has downfalls, they may blame the pastor. This great concern is also seen in Scripture:

> *"And a great windstorm arose, and the waves beat into the boat, so that it was already filling. But He was in the stern, asleep on a pillow. And they awoke Him and said to Him, "Teacher, do You not care that we are perishing?"* (Mark 4:37-38).

The pastor has to be willing to acknowledge the need for assistance to manage the people and administration demands of the church. Dale Marples stated that there are four mistakes pastors make with church finances but these ideas could be generalized to emotional mistakes as well.[13] The first mistake is when pastors have the "Savior" syndrome, and think they can do everything, or that they have to do everything. Pastors may try to do a job that is outside of their calling, but as a pastor, the calling is to "equip the saints for the work of ministry." When one operates outside of or in addition to his or her original scope of ministry, the emotional trauma will increase. It usually leads to the pastor's suffering and the church default, then the congregation is made aware that there is a need.

Overzealousness

An individual's response to the call of ministry is based on a zeal to share the gospel and love of Jesus Christ. One may view this call as a response to Jesus' mandate to the disciples:

> *"Go therefore and make disciples of all nations, baptizing them in the name of the Father and of the Son and of the Holy Spirit, teaching them to observe all things that I have commanded you; and lo, I am with you always, even to the end of the age. Amen"* (Matthew 28:19-10).

As pastors, one is always teaching, discipling, and nurturing. Even after leaving the church and in the comfort of home, pastors are still shepherding a sheep. Most times, there is no idea of when to put an end to the day, because of the commitment to fulfill the cause of Christ.

What happens when the pastor's zeal is extreme and it causes self-destruction? Pastor Cordeiro noted, "A tragic flaw of many leaders is that they cannot recognize their limits or acknowledge their need for others as the demands of work or ministry scale up dramatically."[14] It is tragic because the pastor attempts to be all things to all people, and that is not the plan nor the will of God. Throughout Scriptures, God had leaders to strategically assign individuals to assist with ministry. *"Therefore, brethren, seek out from among you seven men of good reputation, full of the Holy Spirit and wisdom, whom we may appoint over this business; but we give ourselves continually to prayer and the ministry of the word"* (Acts 6:3-4). Furthermore:

The Warning Signs

"And Moses chose able men out of all Israel, and made them heads over the people; rulers of thousands, rulers of hundreds, rulers of fifties, and rulers of tens. So they judged the people at all times; the hard cases they brought to Moses, but they judged every small case themselves" (Exodus 18:25-27).

Pastors who are overzealous find themselves doing more than shepherding sheep. They become easily frustrated with the parishioners, because the church is not growing as fast as envisioned. Therefore, they assume additional ministry opportunities that will give them more exposure and influence. They overcommit themselves and/or the church to fulfill personal goals. Former pastor, Bill Selby stated, "Over-functioning pastors tend to have under-functioning churches." Under-functioning churches have parishioners who do just enough or nothing at all. They operate as a status quo church (e.g. attend worship services on Sunday and a mid-week Bible study).

The overzealous pastor wants to do more for the cause of Christ (e.g. community outreaches; Christian education training; etc.). Most times, the overzealous pastor's intentions are good, but if not properly balanced with quality time in God, it becomes easy to lose oneself in doing ministry and not Christian living. At that time, the focus shifts from soul-winning to egotism.

Egotism

Although this scripture pertains to the office of a bishop, it holds true to the pastorate: *"A bishop then must be blameless, the husband of one wife, temperate, sober-minded, of good behavior, hospitable, able to teach; not given to wine, not violent, not greedy for money, but gentle, not quarrelsome, not covetous"* (1 Timothy 3:2-3). The application is not gender-specific. These godly characteristics apply to all of God's leaders. Christian leaders are a representation of Jesus.

Therefore, their lives are to reflect the characteristics Jesus displayed while living on Earth. Throughout Jesus' ministry, He always reminded people that He represented His Heavenly Father. Jesus said, *"Truly, truly, I say to you, the Son can do nothing of Himself, unless it is something He sees the Father doing; for whatever the Father does, these things the Son does in like manner"* (John 5:19). In each of these Scripture passages, Jesus never operated in ministry to bring fame or accolades to Himself. *"I have glorified you on Earth. I have finished the work which you have given me to do"* (John 17:4). Everything He did was to bring glory to God and to bring the people back to Him.

When a pastor loses sight of this purpose, the spirit of egotism sets in. Egotism is the frame of mind which causes a person to pay too much attention to self, to be conceited, and to become selfish.[15] Robert Louis Stevenson stated, "However grand the truths a preacher taught, however skillful the outward image of the leader, the time comes when the veil falls away and a man is seen by the people as he really is."[16] Egotism exposes an individual's heart.

Unfortunately, in the 21st century, this is what the church and the public is seeing on a daily basis. The spirit of egotism is not in all pastors, but if the news media gets wind of one pastor's downfall or despair, it becomes a general statement for all. Serving in ministry is an honorable assignment, because one could never imagine being chosen to represent God Almighty. When people listen and follow one's leadership, it does increase a person's ego. The Bible shows many unlikely people God used to fulfill His divine plan. He usually called the outcast, the least, and the unfavorable to build the kingdom of God. Scripture states that God used the foolish things to confound the wise, and the weak things to confound the mighty (1 Corinthians 1:27). Therefore, when an individual who was unpopular growing up starts to draw a crowd, it can build self-esteem.

While self-esteem is typically known to be positive and sustaining, the problem with popularity and notoriety is, if unchecked, one will expect it to become a way of life and forget the One who called him. Pastor Joe McKeever listed a few dangers (warning signs) of a minister's inflated ego: "You begin feeling you are something special…You start thinking the church is about you…You start expecting special treatment from everyone…You begin spending money to maintain appearances because people expect us to live in certain ways." McKeever added, "Your family either joins you in this ungodly materialistic lifestyle or resent the blatant hypocrisy and begin resisting church altogether." Pastors may stray from involvement in local pastors' conferences that serve smaller churches, feeling like a "big shot" who has "little in common with them."[17]

If the pastor does not acknowledge and correct these characteristics, the path may lead to the loss of self and everything that was previously important, as her or his church spirals downward. Such ungodly character sheds a negative light on the Christian community. Nonbelievers and unchurched individuals tend to use these few instances as reasons for not having a relationship with Jesus Christ or not attending church services. Yes, these fallen pastors are to represent Christ, but society tends to overlook that pastors are human.

Pastors are only able to serve effectively in ministry through the power and strength of the Holy Spirit. One of the colleagues described the first "challenging" year of his pastorate as follows: "The Lord protected my wife and I through it all and revealed to me that we must have focus and purpose… to lead the flock to the best of our ability through His Strength. Positive results and blessings flowed as a result of our obedience." Pastors serve best in submission to the Holy Spirit, keeping in step with and being led by Him.

Humanity and Limitations of Pastors

Sparsely researched empirically are the mental states of pastors, which can significantly impact churches, communities, and even nations. Rather than viewing emotional and mental health needs and resources as enhancing the shepherding and leading of parishioners, a wave of Christian and pastoral resistance to understanding mental and emotional well-being, and the factors that undermine it, can negatively affect pastors and parishioners seeking assistance. As a result, pastors and their congregations may continue to maintain unrealistic expectations for pastoral leadership. "Traditional conceptions that promote unrealistic expectations of the congregation are likely in turn to foster internal unrealistic expectations kindled by a leader's basic human need to achieve and succeed."[18] With these "internal unrealistic expectations" and a lack of awareness of potential or real threats, pastors may either unnecessarily resist or ignore the competent plentiful resources for pastoral care.

An understanding of the humanity and limitations of pastors, along with the intercession and physical support of the parishioners, are crucial for pastoral well-being. The Apostle Paul called the church the Body of Jesus Christ (1 Corinthians 12) and bodies need each part to systemically coordinate to optimally function. Parishioners must be mindful of their pastors' human limitations and needs. If the pastor overextends, the church may also stretch in unhealthy ways. If the pastor develops a spirit of arrogance, there is a chance some of the parishioners will also walk in arrogance. Ed Stetzer wrote, "Arrogance stifles mission. It redirects the focus of our ministry to us instead of a kingdom focus. The reason this is so dangerous, especially for those in ministry positions, is that it can become a cancer to our ministry."[19] Cancer spreads and cancer kills if left undiagnosed and untreated.

In light of the possibility of this deadly fate, it is important for pastors and churches to partner in pastoral soul care. Pastors are great in encouraging and admonishing the church on the importance of soul care, but it becomes hypocritical if the shepherd doesn't heed to his or her own advice. In the next chapter, I will present the relevance and importance for pastoral soul care.

Endnotes

1. W. Ruben Exantus, Ph.D., *Pastoral Burnout and Leadership Styles* (Bloomington: AuthorHouse, 2012) xvi.
2. Mark Dance, "Pastors are Not Quitting in Droves," LifeWay, 10 Jul. 2019, 23 Nov. 2019 https://facts and trends.net/2019/07/10/pastors-are-not-quitting-in-droves-2/
3. Neil Monaghan and Saeed Ahmed, CNN, "There are now as many Americans who claim no religion as there are evangelicals and Catholics, a survey finds," CNN, 26 Apr. 2019, 23 Nov. 2019 https://www.cnn.com/2019/04/13/us/no-religion-largest-group-first-time-USA-trend/index.html.
4. "Demographics of atheism," Wikipedia, 23 Nov. 2019 https://en.m.wikipedia.org/wiki/demographics_of_atheism.
5. Christina Maslach et al., "Job burnout," Annual Reviews, 2001, 23 Nov. 2019 https://scholar.google.com scholar?q=occupational+burnout+maslach+2001&hl=en&as_sdt=0&as_vis=1&oi=scholar#d=gs qabs&u=%23p%3DjlTbDyOXzl0J.
6. Exantus, 20-21.
7. *Holman Illustrated Bible Dictionary* (Nashville: Holman Bible Publishers, 2003) 1426.
8. Drake De Long-Farmer, "My Experience with Anxiety and How You Can Help Your Pastor," *Expastors,* 6 Aug. 2018, 23 Nov. 2019 http://www.expastors.com/my-experience-with-anxiety-and-how-you-can-help-your-pastor/.
9. Laura Everett, "God Rested: Why Can't Clergy Take a Break" 10 Jan. 2020 https://religionnews.com/2020/01/06/god-rested-why-cant-clergy-take-a-break/
10. Lawrence Robinson et al., "Emotional and Psychological Trauma," *Help Guide,* Oct. 2019, 24 Nov. 2019 https:///www.helpguide.org/articles/ptsd-trauma/coping-with-emotional-and-psychological-trauma.htm.
11. David Keck, *Healthy Churches, Faithful Pastors* (London: Rowman & Littlefield, 2014) 62.
12. Paul David Tripp, *Dangerous Calling* (Wheaton: Crossway, 2012) 30.

13 Dale Marples, "Four Mistakes Pastors Make with Church Finances," Tony Cooke Ministries, 24 Nov. 2019
https://www.tonycooke.org/articles-by-others/mistakes-church-finances/
14 Wayne Cordeiro, *Leading On Empty* (Minneapolis: Bethany House, 2009) 9.
15 *The New Webster's Comprehensive Dictionary of the English Language, Deluxe Edition* (New York: Lexicon Publications, Inc. 1990), 300.
16 J. Oswald Sanders, *Spiritual Leadership* (Chicago: Moody Publishers, 2007) 157.
17 Joe McKeever, "Why Some Preachers Have Oversized Egos. What To Do About It," Joemckeever.com 11 Aug. 2013, 26 Nov. 2019 https://joemckeever.com/we/preachers-ego/.
18 Ellison CW, Mattila WS. The needs of evangelical Christian leaders in the United States. Journal of Psychology and Theology, vol. 11. No. 1, 28–35, 1983.
19 Ed Stetzer, "The Problem with Aarogant Pastors & 5 Ways Not to Be One," *Christianity Today*, 28 Feb. 2013, 26 Nov. 2019 https://www.christianitytoday.com/Ed Stetzer/2013/february/problem-with-arrogant-pastors-5-ways-not-to-be-one.html.

Rise and Fall of Pastors in the 21st Century

Chapter 9
PASTORAL CARE

The stress of pastoral ministry is real and irrefutable. Each day, the lack of soul care is becoming costly to the pastor, family, and the church. Since the beginning of writing this book, it has been reported that two young adult pastors committed suicide. One pastor resigned (because his intense drive was hurting the church staff) and one pastor announced his four-month sabbatical to his church.

Individuals cannot be successful and effective pastors if they do not make time with Jesus. Just as a sheep need a shepherd, so does a pastor need the Great Shepherd. Jesus is the Great Shepherd. Scriptures state:

> *"Now may the God of peace who brought up our Lord Jesus from the dead, that great Shepherd of the sheep, through the blood of the everlasting covenant, make you complete in every good work to do His will, working in you what is well pleasing in His sight, through Jesus Christ, to whom be glory forever and ever. Amen"* (Hebrews 13:20-21).

It is in those times with Him that every good work is being performed. The quality time in God allows the pastor to know what is well-pleasing and displeasing to Him. These moments are times of restoration and replenishment. In these times, one is able to recalibrate both mind and heart.

A pastor who is constantly doing ministry, engrossed in daily church work, and available to everyone, with no time for self or family, will eventually self-destruct. Such pastors may face spiritual, physical, and emotional destruction, and as an end result, major devastation. Pastors reaching this point in ministry may become withdrawn and isolated from family and the church. Tripp stated, "An intentional culture of pastoral separation and isolation is neither biblical nor spiritually healthy."[1] Yet, pastors are not exempt from withdrawal and depression that create unhealthy distance, whether physically or emotionally, from their roles and responsibilities.

Throughout Scripture, the only times Jesus was intentionally separated from people and serving in ministry was when He prayed: *"Now in the morning, having risen a long while before daylight, He went out and departed to a solitary place; and there He prayed"* (Mark 1:35). This prayer was day or night. *"Now it came to pass in those days that He went out to the mountain to pray, and continued all night in prayer to God"* (Luke 6:12). Jesus knew the need to retreat to a solitary place to be restored in God. *"However, the report went around concerning Him all the more; and great multitudes came together to hear, and to be healed by Him of their infirmities. So He Himself often withdrew into the wilderness and prayed"* (Luke 5:15-16). Pastoral withdrawal can be healthy and helpful if one is growing closer to God and not farther from His purpose as a shepherd of His people.

The body has limitation and its effectiveness wanes at a certain point in one's life. Rest is useful in reducing the stress and anxiety. When we take rest, both physically and mentally, we remain away from the stressful situation. It allows the body to calm down and gather some energy as well.[2] Pastors understand the importance of eternal soul care through the decision to receive Jesus Christ as personal Savior, but then may deny physical and mental soul care needed for them to be efficient and effective in their pastoral assignments. This chapter will present the dire need for pastors to make time for their own soul care.

Stepping Back

Physical and mental soul care, needed to be efficient and effective in pastoral assignments, may require stepping back at times. Keck stated:

> While everyone can understand the benefits of having days off during the week or taking vacations, the importance of a pastoral sabbatical allow pastors to step back from years of intense service in order to rest, reflect, and renew. Pastors often report that they need periods of sustained reading, prayer, and learning. They have ideas, notions, and hopes, but the regular guidance of a church precludes their going into things very deeply.[3]

There are many occupations that are demanding of one's schedule, but the pastor's role tends to go beyond the call of duty. A physician is focused on a patient's physical health. A psychologist is concerned about an individual's mental health. A relationship therapist may be concerned about one's emotional health. However, a pastor understands that all three health matters are connected to one's spiritual well-being.

For example, when parishioners become ill, they not only call the doctor, but also call the pastor for prayer. When parishioners experience mental-anguish with life's adversities, they may contact psychologists, but also contact their pastors for guidance. When relationships fail or may have some highlights, the pastor is called to be involved. Across most facets of life, the pastor is usually called and expected to report for duty. Adding each scenario with the number of church members, the pastor is extended beyond capabilities. Taking a step back also involves enlisting adequate support.

The church may have a great leadership team and capable people to provide the same care, but individuals' demands usually supersede what is reasonable. I interviewed a denomination Administrative

Bishop who oversees 140 pastors in a quad-region. I also interviewed a lead pastor and former licensed clinical professional counselor. Currently, he is studying Spiritual Formation for pastors. The lead pastor shared that, in the early stage of his ministry, he felt ill-equipped as a pastor, which caused anxiety. He stated, "I was good with preaching and teaching the Word, but I lacked understanding in counseling people (helping them to see pass hearing Scriptures but applying it to their life's circumstances)." The additional stress is that most members want pastoral care by the senior pastor. In order for pastoral soul care to be successful, there needs to be a four-part partnership: the church and the pastor, the family and the pastor, the friends and the pastor, and the pastor and oneself.

The Church and the Pastor

A known leadership saying is that the mark of a good leader is when the team can function well without the leader being present. Keck claimed that a healthy church setting has three things that make a pastoral sabbatical possible (a) strong lay leadership that can function independently of the pastor; (b) the financial resources to provide for pastoral leadership during the sabbatical time; and (c) a pastor who can be away from the church.[4] Accordingly, all leaders should train their followers to serve as if they will one day be the one in command.

Ministry flows better with a team approach. Servant-leaders do not mind rolling up their sleeves and going into the trenches with their team to serve God and impact people's lives. Sadly, in the 21st century, some pastors actually believe that they can do ministry alone or with one other, but will not offer ministry opportunities to others. Yes, Jesus could have reached some while He was living on Earth, but He knew He could impact many by inviting twelve men to serve as His disciples (Matthew 10:1-4; Mark 3:14-19).

John Maxwell said, "A leader who produces other leaders multiplies their influences."[5] From the twelve men, thousands were added to do kingdom building.

When the parishioners see that the church does not function by the pastor alone, and that others play a key role in the success of ministry, they are less likely to always expect the pastor to be at their beckon call. This allows the pastor some time for self and family. Other leaders can respond to provide the necessary pastoral care, and the parishioner will not feel slighted by the service provided.

The church's financial resource is another major concern to a pastor. It is a known fact that parishioners' commitment in attendance and offerings decline when the pastor is away. The senior pastor I researched, who announced his four-month sabbatical to the church, encouraged the parishioners to remain faithful in their generosity. He emphasized that the church's vision and mission will continue in his absence. The church's various local and world missions still needed to be financially supported.[6] At the same time, most churches provide a stipend to those who assume leadership, give an honorarium to guest preachers, and continue to provide a salary to the pastor who is on sabbatical.

When it comes to church members' faithfulness and commitment in giving, most times, it is not consistent while the pastor is actively present. Nevertheless, the pastor feels the need to stay present to encourage good stewardship. However, it does a pastor well to see that the church flows smoothly, and ministry continues in her or his absence. Dale Wolyniak explained:

> Churches experiencing their own sabbatical alongside that of their minister also gain perspective and understanding of their own calling as a body to be a part of the ministry team. Churches gain a new freedom from old habits of dependency, and enter into a new season of cooperation

with both God and the leader or leaders He has placed among them.[7]

In the relationship between the church and the pastor, the parishioners should be able to envision the pastor's personal, family, and everyday needs experienced beyond the church walls, and encourage the pastor to Sabbath often. The Lead Pastor interviewed previously advised pastors to educate the leadership team on the true life of a pastor and "once they grasp it, they should share it with the congregation." This education encompasses the pastor's needs for spiritual, self, and soul care.

However, pastors serve in roles that do not necessarily encourage the fuller range of self-disclosure, partly because they feel the pressure to set examples for their congregants to follow. Personal self-disclosure flexibility is critical for the well-being of a pastor, because the imbalance in relational connections with others can lead to burnout.[8] Relational imbalances exist when pastors are at the recipient end of self-disclosures, yet do not connect with others in the same ways. Pastors also struggle with self-disclosure or the willingness to discuss their own personal health and needs, because their wellness reflects the foundation of their personal and spiritual identity and is also a vocational prerequisite. As a result of non-disclosure, struggles with other people and with God can continue to undermine spiritual well-being and their relationships with others.

Pastors may not need to self-disclose to be able to benefit from taking a step back, but they must be willing to do so. Sharing his personal experience, the Administrative Bishop stated, "When I pastored my third church, the leadership sent me away every fifth Sunday. They encouraged me to go somewhere, but do not come to the church. Of course, I didn't always heed to it." For a pastor intentionally staying away from the church within the first five years of the pastorate, it can be especially difficult to take a step back. Seasoned pastors have said that those are the honeymoon years and believe the church cannot function without them. Jesus concluded a parable as *"He who is faithful in what is least is faithful also in much; and he who is unjust in what is least is unjust also in much. And if you have not been faithful in what is another man's, who will give you what is your own?"* (Luke 16:10 and 12). It is in these honeymoon years that the relationship between the pastor and the church can develop in appreciation for the pastor's need for care.

As a servant leader, one does not give the air of perfection, but also does not lead recklessly. There are times in everyone's life that personal problems occur. It becomes a disturbance in the flow of ministry when the leader refuses to acknowledge problems and fails to seek assistance to resolve it. Servant-leaders establish a level of trust within their group to make known that there are some personal matters in life that need their primary focus, and encourage the team to continue to work to fulfill the church's mission. Such transparency causes the team members to see the leader's humanness, bringing about a willingness to serve and do whatever is in the best interest of the leader and the church.

The Family and the Pastor

Pastoral soul care saves marriages and sustains family stability. As expressed in Chapter 5, ministry imposes a heavy weight on the pastor's family. A pastor shared:

> I preached five times. It was one of those moments when God's presence was tangibly felt. In fact, after that particular conference, the rest of my year was planned full with preaching all over the country…On my way home after that last sermon amid the divine blessing of that night, my

wife of fifteen years told me she was leaving me.[9]

Far too often, pastoral families are being severed due to pastors' consumption with ministry. Pastors have good intentions to balance family and ministry, but one or both may be neglected for the sake of the other. Family and ministry require the pastor's undivided attention, but the pastor is the final decision-maker of how to prioritize at the appointed time.

Ruth Senter noted, "Ministry couples who avoid burnout are the ones who learned this fact: No matter how long your tenure with any one congregation, your relationship with the people in that congregation is temporary, compared to your relationship with your family."[10] Family is a pastor's first ministry. If the family senses the same fervency and passion to be with them, as shown towards the church, they are less likely to feel threatened by the church. Church will not appear as an enemy to the children. Marshall Shelley shared a pastor's testimony of taking occasional family outings during his children's school holidays and even during school days: "Sometimes we'll take the kids out of school for a special family excursion. Last week, we took Monday and went to see a special display at the museum."[11] The idea expressed was that even school cannot interfere with the family's needs to be together and care for one another.

Pastors must also be able to express what they are experiencing with their families. The Lead Pastor stated, "If the pastor accepts the revelation that he needs soul care, he will be able to educate his spouse and children. The family will be able to dialog often about setting boundaries for them without the church's involvement." The Administrative Bishop's recommendation to families is that the spouse and pastor grab their calendars and block out intentional family days and weeks. They must adhere to those dates (unless there is an emergency).

The Friends and the Pastor

Friends and accountability partners are good sources of pastoral care. These individuals allow the pastor to be transparent about the stress of ministry. The Lead Pastor stated that covenant groups are so important to pastors and their families. He said, "It is good to connect with groups of people unrelated to the church … join a club … something non-pastoral… develop healthy outside church relationships. Relationships that are safe, enriching, and restorative." True friends allow the pastors to complain, cry, and laugh; then, they encourage them to continue in their pastoral calls.

McIntosh and Rima's recommendation to leaders is to find a group of individuals who will agree to help with dealing with difficult decisions, determining directions for life and ministry, navigating through controversial waters, or struggling with inner feelings regarding various issues.[12] The benefit of this soul care is to allow the pastor to release all matters that are consuming the mind. It also helps the pastor to voice aloud visions and desires of the heart. Proverbs 15:22 says, *"Without counsel, plans go awry, but in the multitude of counselors they are established."* The friend or accountability partner will aid in providing sound advice.

The Pastor and Oneself

In order for soul care to be beneficial, a pastor has to be honest with oneself. The pastor has to purposefully stop the work of ministry, find a quiet solitary place, and assess her or his current state. Unfortunately, what tends to occur is that the pastor will thrust beyond one's physical and mental capacity. They will describe it as a passion for ministry or a passion for reaching lost souls, but are perishing within themselves. The longer the shepherd is in denial, the more damaging it becomes to the church and the pastor's family. Dr. Exantus noted, "It is difficult to identify and treat depression in pastors, because they are often depressed before they realized it. Many of them are unaware of the shadows of depression that is haunting their lives and ultimately destroying their ministry."[13] Hence, such denial is the cause of numerous pastors resigning from thriving ministries, frequent media broadcasts of pastors exposed of corrupt or immoral lifestyles, and appalling reports of pastors committing suicide.

When presented with the invitation for soul care, the Lead Pastor stated that there are usually four responses that comes from a pastor. One response may be an "Epiphany." The pastor says, "Oh my, you are exactly right!" Another response could be "Dawning of Ignorance," when the pastor says, "I have no idea what to do with this revelation!" The third response could be "Resistance," when the pastor thinks "I have never done it like this before! I have always gone to the altar and prayed about it." The other response could be "Rejection," when the pastor says, "I am comfortable with the same routine, but I am miserable!"

The Lead Pastor added, "Once the pastor has the epiphany, he needs to give it due diligence and take care of himself. It is not good for the pastor to get the revelation and do not follow through on proper care." It is also not sufficient to hope things will change but do nothing to bring forth the change. Developing a natural routine of Sabbath helps it to occur over time. The Administrative Bishop stated that he encourages pastors to try fifteen minutes to an hour a day to develop a soul care routine. He added that he has seen some pastors making progress, but sadly, he does not hear about a pastor's need for soul care until it is very late.

Pastoral Retirement

In most professions, there is a time limit or requirement to stop. Many believe a pastor should shepherd a church until she or he dies. Retirement can be considered a high or low time in a person's life; in the ministry, retirement might result from another pastoral ministry low. When a congregation has a good pastor, they do not want her or him to leave or retire. This is understandable, because good pastors establish many relationships throughout the life of their pastorate. These relationships oftentimes guide the pastor in the decision of their tenure.

Again, God calls pastors to lead His sheep. Ultimately, God is the one who should determine the length of a pastorate. By and large, I believe this takes place in some cases, but not in most cases. As with other professions, there are questions about retirement and succession. In trying to appreciate a guidepost to determine when it is time for a pastor to step down, all pastors should consider these series of unpopular questions in their pastorate: Who am I preparing to succeed me? To what extent does God want me to carry out the church's vision? Am I being an effective pastor to the church? Am I staying in the pastorate because of fear, comfort, or purpose?

One can search the Scriptures for answers to these questions. For example, what will make this decision easier is when the pastor has a Moses-and-Joshua mentality. When Moses knew his pastorate was ending, he asked God who would succeed him. The LORD said unto Moses, *"Take thee Joshua the son of Nun, a man in whom is the spirit, and lay thine hand upon him… set him before Eleazar the priest, and before all the congregation; and give him a charge in their sight"* (Numbers 27:18-19). God is always progressive and has successors in position to fulfill His will in the church. This is why it is so important for pastors to stay in constant communion with Him. Again, the role of the pastor is a God-assignment, not a self-agenda. Therefore, the pastor should serve with the intent to lead, guide, and nurture His sheep, but at the same time, spiritually-discerning whom God is preparing to succeed her or him.

A pastor's preparation for departure is crucial. During Moses' ministry, Joshua was always near him and faithful to obey his instructions (Exodus 17:9-10; 24:13; 33:11). Now, this concept is not intended until the pastor dies, to prepare men and woman to lead ministry at the appointed time. Without proper successors, pastors may feel they must shepherd forever. No pastor wants to see or hear that their ministry work has vanished or dissolved after their departure.

During the pastoral ministry lows, pastors tend to question their effectiveness as shepherds. If the church's attendance and offering plummets, a pastor carries the burden and sometimes take it personally. In *Charisma Leader,* Joe McKeever advised a pastor resign, "when the pastor whose support from the congregation has dwindled away to next to nothing. There is no point in trying to lead people who will not follow."[14] Others disagree. Most people who shepherded a church for some time know that ministry is seasonal and transitional. During this low time of ministry, the pastor should seek the Lord for guidance. One can reflect on the idea of a season of reassessment and if the church is under spiritual construction. One might ask: Have I taken the church as far as I can go?

In this self-reflective process, a pastor might ask if staying in the pastorate stems from fear, comfort, or purpose. Individuals may stay in a position because it is familiar and they are afraid to step out of their comfort zone (especially those who are fulltime and tenured). The pastor may believe that another church will not be sensitive to personal time and family. If the idea of becoming a bi-vocational pastor is presented, she or he may believe that it would be difficult to shepherd a church and maintain another position outside of the church. The pastor begins to question her or his loyalty to the parishioners and to the employer. These thoughts tend to stem from fear, but God encourages us to trust Him and not our own understanding (Proverbs 3:5-6).

As previously noted, there are some pastors who loved the comfort of shepherding the same church for over thirty or more years, even if the church and its ministry was unfruitful and ineffective in the community. The parishioners' spiritual lives may grow stagnant and comfortably compromising with the world's standard. These pastors may believe that "all is right" with the world and their church, but it contradicts the Word of God. Throughout Scripture, God always allowed friction to take place in the body of Christ to keep His people dispersed to spiritually impact communities (Genesis 11:8; Esther 3:8; Acts 8).

If a pastor knows his purpose for shepherding a church, one can persevere and press past the ministry lows and create ministry highs (for both self and the church). When serving the people became too much for King David, he learned to encourage himself in the Lord: *"And David was greatly distressed; for the people spake of stoning him, because the soul of all the people was grieved, every man for his sons and for his daughters: but David encouraged himself in the LORD his God"* (1 Samuel 30:6). Establishing sabbatical time to allow God to redirect, recalibrate, and restore can prepare a pastor for the church's next season or phase of ministry.

Overall, pastoral retirement can represent another form of soul care, but it does require proper planning. In seeking a successor for the church, a pastor can also pursue a retirement package established with the church. The income and lifestyle changes when there is no longer a steady flow of financial resources or place of residence changes, if the pastor and his family lived in a parsonage. Edward Bratcher noted, "As retirement approaches, most pastors find it helpful not only to prepare to leave fulltime ministry but also to live a retired life." He further stated that financial preparation for retirement is a lifelong endeavor.[15] Thus the need for pastors to find Sabbath rest in the Lord; He will be the One to let them know when their pastoral season is ending, and the time of relaxation or the choice of other ministry options is drawing near.

In summary, too often in the 21st century, we are seeing constant reports of pastors deteriorating and dying in ministry. This is totally contrary to God's intent for pastors. Just as God calls the shepherd to lead the sheep into an eternal relationship with Him, He also wants the pastor to purposefully establish Sabbath rest in Him. Yes, we are in the last days (as written in Scripture) and the gospel needs to be made known to all mankind; yet if God created the heavens and Earth in six days and rested on the seventh day, why should not pastors do likewise?

In the final chapter, I will summarize the key points of the rise and fall of 21st century pastors. I will provide further acknowledgements of my colleagues and informants who aided in my research. I will leave the pastoral reader with practical methods of capitalizing on the highs of ministry, identifying and discerning the lows, and intentionally establishing soul care plans that will protect them from reaching burnout, feeling inadequate, and losing self and family. I will leave pastoral families and church members with ideas to protect their pastors and their well-being. I will conclude with a final insight of the life of a 21st century pastor as God intended.

Endnotes

1. Paul David Tripp, *Dangerous Calling* (Wheaton: Crossway, 2012) 70.
2. Importance of Rest for Good Health," *Fitness Gear & Equipment*, 20 Apr. 2011, 15 Dec. 2019 https://fitness-gear-equipment.knoji.com/importance-of-rest-for-good-health/.
3. David Keck, *Healthy Churches, Faithful Pastors* (London: Rowman & Littlefield, 2014) 142
4. Ibid, 142.
5. Peter Economy, "44 Inspiring John C. Maxwell Quotes for Leadership Success," *Inc.*, 5 Jun. 2015, 15 Dec. 2019 https://www.inc.com/peter-economy/44-inspiring-john-c-Maxwell-quotes-that-will-take-you-to-leadership-success.html.
6. Selah." YouTube, sermon by Rev. Dr. Howard-John Wesley, 1 Dec. 2019, https://youtu.be/rbnsDoXphUo.
7. Dale Walyniak, "Sabbaticals for Ministers: The Benefits for Pastors and Congregations," *Focus On the Family,* 16 Dec 2019 http://media.focusonthefamily.com/pastoral/pdf/PAS_Sabbaticals.pdf
8. Salwen, Erik D et al. "Self-Disclosure and Spiritual Well-Being in Pastors Seeking Professional Psychological Help." *Pastoral psychology* vol. 66,4 (2017): 505-521. doi:10.1007/s11089-017-0757-1
9. Zack Eswine, *The Imperfect Pastor* (Wheaton: Crossway, 2015) 24.
10. Ruth Senter, "A Spouse's Choice of Role," *Leadership Handbook of Management and Administration* (Grand Rapids: Baker Books, 1994) 59.
11. Marshall Shelley, "Responsibility to Family Members," *Leadership Handbook of Management and Administration* (Grand Rapids: Baker Books, 1994) 57.
12. Gary L. McIntosh and Samuel D. Rima, *Overcoming the Dark Side of Leadership* (Grand Rapids: Baker Books, 2007) 209.
13. W. Ruben Exantus, Ph.D., *Pastoral Burnout and Leadership Styles* (Bloomington: AuthorHouse, 2012) 96.
14. Joe McKeever, "When Should A Pastor Resign?" *Charisma Leader,* 25 Jul. 2016, 14 Jan. 2020 https://ministrytodaymag.com/life/relationships/23029-when-should-a-pastor-resign

15 James Berkley, General Editor, *Leadership Handbook of Management Administration* (Grand Rapids: Baker Books, 1994) 106-107.

Chapter 10
CONCLUSION

The pastoral call is a copious assignment. It is not a work for the faint-hearted or apathetic. Pastoring in the 21st century is not a popular career nor an appealing position. It is a God-ordained appointment. This appointment requires an individual to care, to guide, and to protect God's sheep. Due to the high demand of this esteem position, one has to maintain an intimate relationship and is in constant communication with God the Father. If the individual ceases from this relationship, the most likely result is to burn out, resign, or expire at the pinnacle of ministry.

Although God's original intent for pastors is to tend to His sheep, many 21st century pastors have come to realize that there is much more entailed in that assignment. In times past, ministerial students were trained in reading and properly understanding Scriptures, so they could rightly propagate the Bible to an audience. From my research, we have heard pastors state that their seminary education and theological training did not prepare them for extensive church administration or conflict resolution with parishioners. Such lack of knowledge and training have caused extreme stress on these pastors. Their seminary education and theological training did not prepare them for the personal and mental effects that ministry would have on them and their families.

Since pastoral ministry is multi-faceted, it has such a poignant effect on one's life and family. As the world remains transitional, pastors need to be more apt and equipped to minister to their congregation and community without becoming despaired and losing themselves and families in the midst of ministry. Additional courses and trainings can serve as a precaution to protect the well-being of pastoral colleagues. I recommend that additional courses should be offered in seminary and theological education, such as Biblical Conflict Resolution, Shepherding a Degenerative Society, Ministry and Family Relations, and Harmonizing Pastoral Ministry.

Biblical Conflict Resolution will teach pastors the biblical and practical methodology of applying Matthew 5:23-25 and Matthew 18:15-17. This course may relieve some of the pressures of holding on to offenses, which as a result, erode a pastor's heart. Shepherding a Degenerative Society will equip pastors in dealing with the social phenomena that are affecting the Christian community. This course will assist pastors to remain biblically-sound, yet relative to the congregation, without compromising the faith. Ministry and Family Relations will train pastors and families how to incorporate the work of ministry while maintaining a stable home. This training will allow pastoral families to experience the benefits of serving in ministry together versus separately. Harmonizing Pastoral Ministry will teach pastors to establish a balanced life (personal, family, and ministry). This course causes the pastor to see the importance of Soul Care.

Those called to the pastorate do not expect that their families would need to develop coping mechanisms when dealing with church members. My research has shown that ministry involves an entire family. Twenty-first century pastors have to be intentional with their families. They have to be purposeful in having family talks about ministry and its demands on them. Pastors have to be reminded that their first ministry is their family, and then the church follows. Pastors must maintain a First Timothy 3:5 principle: *If a man cannot rule his own house, how shall he take care of the church of God?*

In my research, I have found limited material on pastoral family involvement in ministry. There is a plethora of information written to pastors on the importance of establishing quality times with the family, but there is little information on how to prepare and transition a family into ministry. Family quality time is crucial for stability, but just as critical is teaching the family how to enjoy serving in ministry.

Due to limited material on pastoral families, the information provided tended to focus on the husband being the pastor and his wife being the supporter. Absent was material related to women serving as senior or lead pastor, with the husband as the supporter. In my research, I interviewed four female lead pastors. Two of the four women are married and their spouses serve in the ministry alongside them. I attempted to interview one husband to provide another perspective to the effects of pastoral ministry on the family. Unfortunately, he chose not to do so, thus there was an element of bias from the perspective of female spouses. The teen and adult children who informed this study appeared largely to enjoy the work of ministry. The assumption that churches' expectations causes a negative view of ministry to children was not the case with the group I interviewed, despite some expressed concerns. These pastoral families were intentional about maintaining a proper balance between ministry and family.

I have observed that all pastors can recall their ministry highs, and the first high was the day of their initial sermon. Once they pressed past the fear of the audience's responses and allowed themselves to rest in the help of the Holy Spirit, they all stated that they were ready for the next ministry opportunity. When asked about their ministry lows, the common overall response dealt with their pastorate and their interactions with the parishioners. These pastors expressed the emotional pain of overextending themselves for the sake of the parishioners' well-being and the end result can vary from no spiritual growth to deciding to leave the church. Each pastor understood that people will depart from the ministry, but emphatically stated that the separation would still be painful.

There is limited information to address the pastors' emotional stressors when parishioners separate from a church. The material provided was written with the assumption that all pastors are possessors or have a hoarder's complex syndrome. I have found in both research, and personally as an associate pastor, that the separation experience is similar to those of parents and children. There are times when children believe they are grown and anxiously move out of the home before maturation. The parents protectively attempt to communicate and warn them of the dangers and consequences of leaving home too early. Unfortunately, a child may not heed the advice and leaves. As a result, the parent is grieved. Then, there are other instances when the child is mature and ready to leave the home, and the parents are supportive, but it does not ward off the sadness of separation. The joys and convenience of having the child home are grand, but it still hurts to see the child go.

I recommend further research to be conducted on the stages of pastor-parishioner relationships. I believe this is an innate relationship that has never had a full-scope study to determine the effects that it has on both parties. I agree that some pastors have a possessive spirit and tend to perceive separation as rejection, but there are many pastors who have embraced the shepherd's call and become heavy-hearted when parishioners leave (especially if the separation is dysfunctional).

In my research, I have found that most pastors do not heed to the warning signs of destruction until their bodies began to deteriorate, families are fragmented, the church is dissolving, and their immoral character is exposed. As the Administrative Bishop stated, "The need for soul care is not recognized until it is too late." The aim of the book was to encourage pastors to embrace their shepherd's call, to be aware of leadership threats, and to move forward in a regiment of soul care to sustain their life.

I have concluded that the effectiveness of pastoral and church leadership requires soul care. Soul care is the pastor intentionally

Conclusion

establishing rest and relaxation time for oneself. Daily, there are media reports of the immoral conduct of a prominent pastor, the suicide of a mega-pastor, or a pastor's lavish living at the expense of the church. These media reports have heightened awareness of pastors' successes, failures, or demises. Unfortunately, this plight will not cease if pastors continue to forget that they are sheep and that they need to spend time with the Chief Shepherd, Jesus Christ. Just as pastors are to teach sheep to find rest, they must trust to do the same for themselves.

As previously stated, since the beginning of this book, it has been reported that two young adult pastors have committed suicide, one pastor resigned because his intense drive was hurting the church staff, and one pastor announced his four-month sabbatical to his church. I am confident that there are numerous unreported pastoral fatalities and indiscretions. My hope in writing is to bring an awareness to this heart-wrenching epidemic in the Christian community and to cease any future incidences from occurring.

My conviction is that pastors would remember whom they are serving and why they were called to ministry. They must accept that the ministry call was never about them, but about Christ and His love for all mankind. Therefore, when the weight of ministry becomes overwhelming, they have to return back to the One-in-Charge, God the Father. The method of returning is called Sabbath Rest. It is at this time that God is able to restore, replenish, and refocus the individual to better serve His sheep.

My book addressed the questions and the threats that caused the rise and fall of pastors in the 21st century. Revealed were biblical, theological, and practical principles to equip pastors to be aware of the threats that causes a decline in their leadership. Addressed in the research was the assessments of society's misunderstanding, misconception, and misinterpretation of the role of the pastor, as these concepts pertained to a pastor's rise and fall. The interviews, questionnaires, and surveys exposed the realities of 21st century pastors' successes and failures in life, family, and ministry. I derived from my peers that soul care is crucial for the survival in the pastorate.

I end with the question: If the pastors do not learn to make time to rest in the Lord and continue to perish, who will be left to care for God's sheep? The reviewed published articles and statistics from 2000 to present were indicators that soul care is necessary in preserving the sanctity of marriage, family stability, mental stability, and physical, as well as, spiritual well-being of a pastor. Finally, my prayer is that parishioners will proactively and earnestly pray for their pastors as the Apostle Paul encouraged the church:

> *"I exhort therefore, that, first of all, supplications, prayers, intercession, and giving thanks, be made for all men; for kings, and for all that are in authority; that we may lead a quiet and peaceable life in all godliness and honesty"* (1 Timothy 2:1-2).

Bibliography

Ahmed, Saeed and Neil Monaghan.
"There are now as many Americans who claim no religion as there are evangelicals and Catholics, a survey finds." *CNN*. 26 Apr. 2019. https://www.cnn.com/2019/04/13/us/no-religion-largest-group-first-time-USA-trend/index.html. Accessed 23 Nov. 2019

Allen, Jason K.
"Eight Tips for Beginning Preachers." *Jasonkallen.com.* 11 May 2016. https://jasonkallen.com/2016/05/eight-tips-for-beginning-preachers/. Accessed 27 Aug. 2019.

"A Solutions-Focused Ministry." *Pastoral Care, Inc.* 17 Sept. 2019. https://www.pastoralcareinc.com. Accessed 27 Aug. 2019.

Austin, Steven
From Pastor to a Psych Ward. Middletown, Steve Austin, 2016.

Banks, William L.
Pastor's Pal. Fort Washington, CLC Publications, 2007.

Beard, M.
"Boundaries: Definition and Types of Boundaries." *Cross Roads.* 8 Dec. 2016. https://crossroadsindy.com/counseling-blog/couples-and-marriage/boundaries-definition-and-types-of-boundaries Accessed. 29 Oct. 2019

Belet, Daniel
"Enhancing Leadership Skills with Action Learning." *Development and Learning in Organizations: An International Journal,* vol. 2016, no. 30, 2016. https://www.emerald.com/insight/content/doi/10.1108/DLO-06-2016-0049/full/html Accessed 22 Dec. 2019.

Berkley, James D.
General Editor. *Leadership Handbook of Management and Administration.* Grand Rapids, Baker Books, 1994.

Bradley, Jayson D.
"10 Qualities Church Members Expect in a Pastor." *Ministry Advice.* 4 Jan. 2017. https://ministryadvice.com/pastoral-expectations/. Accessed 17 Sept. 2019

Branaugh, Matthew
"5 Church Administration Issues You Need to Know—But Didn't Learn

in Seminary."
https://www.christianitytoday.com/pastors/2016/july-web-exclusives/5-church-administration-issues-you-need-to-know-but-didnt-l.html Accessed 12 Jan. 2019

Chappell, Paul
"Five Reasons Pastors Should Grow in Administrative Skills." *Paulchappell.com.* 23 Apr 2018.
https://paulchappell.com/2018/04/23/five-reasons-pastors-should-grow-in-administrative-skills/. Accessed 31 Aug. 2019

Chilton, Brian G.
"Pastors, Don't Neglect Your Family for Your Ministry." *Christian Post.* 15 Oct. 2019.
https://www.christianpost.com/voice/pastors-dont-neglect-your-family-for-your-ministry.html. Accessed 3 Sept. 2019

Cordeiro, Wayne
Leading On Empty. Minneapolis, Bethany House, 2009.

Dance, Mark
"Pastors are Not Quitting in Droves." *LifeWay.* 10 Jul. 2019.
https://factsandtrends.net/2019/07/10/pastors-are-not-quitting-in-droves-2/. Accessed 23 Nov. 2019

Davis, Jim
"5 Signs You're an At-Risk Pastor." *The Gospel Coalition.* 8 Oct. 2019.
https://www.thegospelcoalition.org/article/5-signs-you're-at-risk-pastor? Accessed 19 Nov. 2019

Davis, Ken
7 Keys to Lead Successful House Groups. Middletown, Elevitamedia, 2015.

De Long-Farmer, Drake
"My Experience with Anxiety and How You Can Help Your Pastor." *Expastors.* 6 Aug. 2018.
http://www.expastors.com/my-experience-with-anxiety-and-how-you-can-help-your-pastor/. Accessed 23 Nov. 2019

"Difference between Bible College and Seminary," *Difference.guru,*
https://www.google.com/amp/s/difference.guru/difference-between-bible-college-and-seminary/amp/. Accessed 10 Sep. 2019.

Doriani, Dan
"3 Occupational Hazards for Pastors." *The Gospel Coalition.* 23 Jul. 2015.
https:///www.thegospelcoalition.org/article/3-occupational-hazards-for-pastors/. Accessed 19 Nov. 2019

Bibliography

Economy, Peter
"44 Inspiring John C. Maxwell Quotes for Leadership Success." *Inc.* 5 Jun. 2015.
https://www.inc.com/peter-economy/44-inspiring-john-c-Maxwell-quotes-that-will-take-you-to-leadership-success.html. Accessed 15 Dec. 2019

Edmondson, Ron
"4 Suggestions for Balancing the Highs and Lows of Ministry." *Church Leaders.* 10 Aug. 2018.
https://churchleaders.com/pastors/pastor-articles/330674-4-suggestions-balancing-the-highs-and-lows-of-ministry-Ron-Edmondson.html. Accessed 4 Nov. 2019

Eswine, Zack
The Imperfect Pastor. Wheaton, Crossway, 2015.

Exantus, W. Ruben, Ph.D.
Pastoral Burnout and Leadership Styles. Bloomington, Author House, 2012.

Filat, Vasile
"Can You Preach Unprepared, Only Guided by the Holy Spirit?" *Christian Moldova.md.* 28 Oct. 2017.
https://moldovacrestina.md/en/can-you-preach-unprepared-only-guided-by-the-holy-spirit/. Accessed 29 Aug. 2019

Gangel, Kenneth O.
Feeding & Leading. Grand Rapids, Baker Books, 1989.

Hall, Steve
"Replenish Participant's Guide." *DELMARVA-DC Church of God.* Columbia, Church of God, 2019.

Hancock, Andrew
"Pastoral Training in the Local Church." *Amicalled.com.* 15 Mar. 2018.
https://amicalled.com/2018/03/pastoral-training-local-church/. Accessed 16 Sept. 2019

Hart, Ray E.
"CARE: Ministry and the Family." *Ministerial Internship Program.* Cleveland, Church of God Ministerial: Development School of Ministry, 2007.

Hart, Ray E.
"Growing Up in a Pastor's Home." *Ministerial Internship Program.* Cleveland, Church of God Ministerial Development School of Ministry, 2007.

Hayes, Justin L.,
"An Analysis of Education and Experience in Pastoral Leadership Development" (2015). Ed.D. Books, 78, https://pdfs.semanticscholar.

org/c16e/93f7611f8edcd23a1a5cac8bfd3f69a13a88.pdf Accessed 13 Jan. 2020.

Hernandez, Roger
"When Ministry Hurts Your Family." *Christianity Today.* Feb. 2014. https://www.christianitytoday.com/pastors/2014/february-online-only/when-ministry-hurts-your-family.html. Accessed 15 Oct. 2019.

Hodges, Phil and Ken Blanchard.
Lead Like Jesus. Nashville, Thomas Nelson, 2005.

Holman Illustrated Bible Dictionary. Nashville, Holman Bible Publishers, 2003.

Howell, James C., Craig T. Kocher, and Jason Byassee, Editors.
Mentoring For Ministry: The Grace of Growing Pastors. Eugene: Cascade Books, 2017.

"Importance of Rest for Good Health."
Fitness Gear & Equipment. 20 Apr. 2011. https://fitness-gear-equipment.knoji.com/importance-of-rest-for-good-health/. Accessed 15 Dec. 2019

"Is a Formal Bible Education Necessary for a Pastor?"
Christian Truth. https://www.compellingtruth.org/pastor-education.html. Accessed 10 Sept. 2019.

Jones, Aaron R.
The Pastor's Intercessor: Devotional Prayers for Your Pastor. Kearney, Morris Publishing, 2011.

Keck, David
Healthy Churches, Faithful Pastors. London, Rowman & Littlefield, 2014.

Lawless, Chuck
"8 reasons long-term pastors still fail." *The Christian Post.* 11 Nov. 2019. https://www.christianpost.com/voice/8-reasons-long-term-pastors-still-fail.html. Accessed 12 Jan. 2020.

Linder, Andrew S.
"7 Practical Keys to Balancing Family, Work & Ministry." Godlyparent.com. 21 Mar. 2016. http://andrewscottlinder.com/balancing-family-work-and-ministry. Accessed 24 Sept. 2019.

Livingstone, Josie Sison
"The Duties of an Evangelist." *Classroom.* 29 Sept. 2017. https://classroom.synonym.com/the-duties-of-an-evangelist-12080929.html. Accessed 24 Aug. 2019.

Marples, Dale
"Four Mistakes Pastors Make with Church Finances." *Tony Cooke Ministries.* https://www.tonycooke.org/articles-by-others/mistakes-church-finances/.

Bibliography

Accessed 24 Nov. 2019.

Maslach, Christina, et al. "Job Burnout." *Annual Reviews.* 2001. https://www.annualreviews.org/doi/abs/10.1146/annurev.psych.52.1.397. Accessed 12 Jan. 2020.

McKeever, Joe
"7 Expectations Every Congregation Should Have for Their Pastor." *Crosswalk.* 30 Nov. 2016.
https://www.crosswalk.com/blogs/joe-mckeever/7-expectations-every-congregation-should-have-for-their-pastor.html. Accessed 17 Sept. 2019

McKeever, Joe
"Why Some Preachers Have Oversized Egos. What To Do About It." Joemckeever.com. 11 Aug. 2013.
https://joemckeever.com/we/preachers-ego/. Accessed 26 Nov. 2019

"Ministry-Related Burnout and Stress Coping Mechanisms Among Assemblies of God-Ordained Clergy in Minnesota."
Research Gate. Aug. 2016.
https://www.researchgate.net/publications_Among_Assemblies_of_God_Clergy_in_Minnesota/amp. Accessed 12 Oct. 2019

Morris, H. Jack
"The Superhuman Pastor." *Ministry Magazine.* Jan. 2019.
https://www.ministrymagazine.org/archive/2019/01/The-superhuman-pastor. Accessed 11 Nov. 2019

Morris, Philip and Mary
Uncharted Waters: The Life & Ministry of Raymond E. Crowley. Cleveland, Pathway Press, 2014.

The New Webster's Comprehensive Dictionary of the English Language,
Deluxe Edition. New York: American International Press, 1990.

Nieuwhof, Carey
"5 Reasons Pastors Fail Morally (And What to Watch For in Your Own Life)." *Careynieuwhof.com.* 12 Aug. 2014.
https://careynieuwhof.com/5-reasons-pastors-fail-morally-and-what-to-watch-for-in-your-own-life/. Accessed 19 Nov. 19

Nieuwhof, Carey
"Some Thoughts About the Recent Exit of Two Megachurch Pastors." Sep 2016.
https://Carey Nieuwhof.com/some-thoughts-about-the-recent-exit-of-two-megachurch-pastors/. Accessed 12 Nov. 2019

Presser, Stanley, and Mike Chavez
"Is Religious Service Attendance Declining?" Journal for the Scientific

Study of Religion, vol. 46, no. 23, 2007. https://onlinelibrary.wiley.com/doi/abs/10.1111/j.1468-5906.2007.00367.x Accessed 9 Jan. 2020.

Rath, Tom
Strengths Based Leadership. New York, Gallup Press, 2008.

Rima, Samuel D. and Gary L. McIntosh
Overcoming the Dark Side of Leadership. Grand Rapids, Baker Books, 2007.

Robinson, Lawrence, et al.
"Emotional and Psychological Trauma." *Help Guide.* Oct. 2019. https:///www.helpguide.org/articles/ptsd-trauma/coping-with-emotional-and-psychological-trauma.html. Accessed 24 Nov. 2019

Robinson, Natasha Sistrunk
"Answering the Call of God." *ChristianityToday.com.* 9 Jan. 2013. https://www.christianitytoday.com/women-leaders/2013/January/answering-call-of-god.html?paging+off. Accessed 24 Aug. 2019

Sanders, J. Oswald
Spiritual Leadership. Chicago, Moody Publishers, 2007.

"Selah." YouTube sermon by Rev. Dr. Howard-John Wesley. 1 Dec. 2019. https://youtu.be/rbnsDoXphUo. Accessed 14 Jan. 2020.

Senter, Ruth
"A Spouse's Choice of Role." *Leadership Handbook of Management and Administration.* Grand Rapids, Baker Books, 1994.

Shelley, Marshall
"Responsibility to Family Members." *Leadership Handbook of Management and Administration.* Grand Rapids, Baker Books, 1994.

Sprinkles, Preston
"4 Ways the Modern Church Looks Nothing Like the Early Church." *Relevant Magazine.* 12 Nov. 2019. https://relevantmagazine.com/god/4-ways-modern-church-looks-nothing-early-church/. Accessed 15 Nov. 2019

"Statistics in the Ministry."
Ministry Missing Link. https://www.pastotalcareinc.com/statistics/. Accessed 4 Oct. 2019.

Stetzer, Ed
"Should Churches Have Multiple Worship Service Styles? Consumerism or Contextualization?" *Christianity Today.* 27 Sept. 2011. https://www.christianitytoday.com/edstetzer/2011/september/should-churches-have-multiple-worship-service-styles.html. Accessed 15 Nov. 2019

Bibliography

Stetzer, Ed
"The Problem with Arrogant Pastors & 5 Ways Not to Be One." *Christianity Today*. 28 Feb. 2013.
https://www.christianitytoday.com/EdStetzer/2013/february/problem-with-arrogant-pastors-5-ways-not-to-be-one.html. Accessed 26 Nov. 2019

Strong, James
The New Strong's Exhaustive Concordance of the Bible. Nashville, Thomas Nelson Publishers, 1990.

Sullivan, Debra
"Adrenaline Rush: Everything You Should Know." *Healthline*. 1 Nov. 2018. https://www.healthline.com/health/adrenaline-rush#causes. Accessed 2 Nov. 2019

Sung, Joong Kim
"Development of Pastoral Administrative Leadership Scale Based on the Theories of Educational Leadership," Jan. 9, 2020.
https://www.tandfonline.com/doi/full/10.1080/23311975.2019.1579963

Taylor, Justin
"30 Years Ago Today: How God Called John Piper to Become a Pastor." *The Gospel Coalition*. 14 Oct. 2009.
https://www.thegospelcoalition.org/blogs/Justin-Taylor/30-years-ago-today-how-god-called-john-piper-to-become-a-pastor/.
Accessed 24 Aug. 2019

"Top Theological Seminaries." *Church Relevance*.
https://churchrelevance.com/resources/theological-seminaries-list/.
Accessed 10 Sept. 2019

Tripp, Paul David
Dangerous Calling. Wheaton, Crossway, 2012.

Twenge, Jean M et al.
"Generational and time period differences in American adolescents' religious orientation, 1966-2014." *PloS one* vol. 10,5 e0121454. 11 May. 2015, doi:10.1371/journal.pone.0121454

Walyniak, Dale
"Sabbaticals for Ministers: The Benefits for Pastors and Congregations." *Focus On the Family*.
http://media.focusonthefamily.com/pastoral/pdf/PAS_Sabbaticals.pdf.
Accessed 16 Dec. 2019

Warren, Rick
The Purpose-Driven Church. Grand Rapids, Zondervan, 1995.

Westing, Harold J.
   Church Staff Handbook. Grand Rapids, Krefeld Publications, 1997.
"Why Pastors Need Mentors and How to Find One."
   Church Fuel. 27 Feb. 2019.
   https://churchleaders.com/pastors/pastor-articles/345232-why-pastors-need-a-mentor-and-how-to-find-one.html. Accessed 16 Sept. 2019

About the Author

Dr. Sharon D. Jones serves as Human Resource Pastor at New Hope Church of God of Waldorf, Inc. She works alongside her husband and senior pastor, Bishop Aaron R. Jones. She oversees the human resource functions of the church and outreach. Sharon is an Associate Certified Coach and member of the International Coach Federation (ICF). She and her husband are Certified SYMBIS Facilitators.

Sharon earned a Doctorate in Christian Leadership and Management from Logos University in Jacksonville, Florida. She has over twenty years of experience in human resource management and development; secondary and undergraduate education; and marketing and sales. She serves on the Church of God's Regional Ministerial Internship Program Board, Women's Ministry Board, and the Youth & Discipleship Board. She conducts monthly morning devotions with the Catherine Foundation Pregnancy Center in Waldorf, Maryland. Sharon is the Vice President of the International Kingdom Women's Coalition, Inc. (IKWC) in Upper Marlboro, Maryland.

Like the Apostle Paul, Sharon counts all those things as dung when she compares it to her life in Christ Jesus. Her life's motto is "Enjoying Life in Christ." Sharon answered the call to ministry in 2000 and became an Ordained Minister in 2002. In 2015, she authored another book entitled, *R.E.W.A.R.D.: Restoring Every Woman's Adrenaline Rush to Disciple.*

www.ingramcontent.com/pod-product-compliance
Lightning Source LLC
Chambersburg PA
CBHW072017110526
44592CB00012B/1349